Seeing
Beyond Illusions

Seeing
Beyond Illusions

Freeing Ourselves
from Ego, Guilt,
and the Belief
in Separation

David Ian Cowan

WEISERBOOKS
San Francisco, CA / Newburyport, MA

This edition first published in 2015 by Weiser Books
Red Wheel/Weiser, LLC
With offices at:
665 Third Street, Suite 400
San Francisco, CA 94107
www.redwheelweiser.com

ISBN: 978-1-57863-574-0

Library of Congress Cataloging-in-Publication Data available upon request.

Cover design by Jim Warner
Cover photograph © Asaf Eliason/shutterstock
Interior by Maureen Forys, Happenstance Type-O-Ram
Typeset in Goudy Old Style and Din

Printed in the United States of America.
EBM
10 9 8 7 6 5 4 3 2 1

I dedicate this work to my mother, Dorothy Alberta Cowan (1925-2014) whose love, devotion and prayers will always be a guiding light in my life. Thanks, Mom, you're the best.

Contents

Foreword

Ken Carey

The simple prose and vivid images evoked in David Ian Cowan's most recent offering do not so much "teach us" as help us remember what we have always known—the spiritual genius behind the structure of our Universe, Life! Beauteous Life, brimming over with the very celestial music that brings us into being, with new sounds on new frequencies that gently blow away the disharmonious lies of separation that obscure our vision of the perfection that exists all around us.

And forgiveness! The sections of this book—thankfully long—that deal with the topic surpass all that I have read before, both in substance, scope, depth, and implication. And surprisingly, they do so in simple, clear, and easy-to-understand language. Of all the material I have encountered on the topic, including my own writing, I would recommend this book to anyone even remotely interested in a permanent elevation of consciousness, the healing of self or a loved one, and oh so many other breakthroughs in an array of fields. It is not overstatement to say that, when understood and practiced, *forgiveness*, as so thoroughly explored in this book, is our ticket to a New Heaven and a New Earth, and most of all, to the unification of Creator and Creation.

I began reading *Seeing Beyond Illusions* as I would any other book, when gradually a feeling crept over me that brought me up short: *It was as if I were reading my own thoughts as they instantaneously appeared before me.* Or was the smooth flow of meaning in the words causing my thoughts to recede behind a river's shorelines and lazy waters in a hazy but deliciously beckoning direction? Before long, my plans for the evening receded into the background. Hours passed. Awareness of turning pages, the knowledge I was reading, faded into smooth, strong thought-currents that carried me along.

Yes, a river it was. It could have been a preference of my mind, or the manner in which it is being nurtured, but I remember *Seeing Beyond Illusions* more visually than conceptually, more in terms of the river reflections still before me than the poetry that triggered them. Before you flip to chapter 1 and begin reading this extraordinary material for yourself, a few more words on my take.

The river I was riding was relatively straight and calm, about seventy-five yards wide and wholly without rapids. I was traveling through the One Moment, the One Presence, the Alpha and Omega of All That Is. Vegetation along the shoreline was beautiful beyond superlatives, and even as I looked to left and right I recognized the terrain as painting from my own brush. I was drawing the scenery both in and into my attentive field; indeed, I was creating it. Turning my head upstream, my chest released tensions I had not consciously known I was carrying. Subtle new sounds and songs in soft and ever-changing languages drifted through my mind, new fragrances enticed me from among the trees that lined the shore, yet it was when I turned to observe the shorelines past that I was suddenly engulfed in joy. I'm not even going to try to describe this. Along both banks of the river, as far as I could see, was the same perfect, lush—and oh so beautiful—vegetation that I had been creating in that very present moment along the shores to either side.

Behind me, upstream, were no blank empty stretches of desert to signify my lapses into cultural beliefs. The dark ages while I had dreamed my troubled dreams showed only the same entwined vegetation of perfect love and perfect truth of that which I had created consciously.

So even while I was sleeping the sleep of an individual apart from God and Nature, *I/You/We's* most Primal Creative Power had penetrated the shell of my illusions to create, through the microscopic, myopic me, *everything* My Eternal Spirit had wanted to be.

No, it was all as beautiful and whole as what I had and still am creating consciously. But even during those years when ego had dethroned Spirit from the decision-making citadel of my brain, my Spirit, *our Whole Spirit,* was still ensuring the perfection of all things. Everything my ego showed me was illusion. This was quite possibly the greatest lasting gift I have taken away from this book.

KEN CAREY
March, 2014

Introduction

When I read a book I am certainly absorbing information, but at the same time, from a different part of my mind, I am absorbing essence. This is the word I use to describe the subtle feeling that a book offers beneath the concepts it describes. Although I most likely won't recall "chapter and verse" what was said, I can still tell you today how a certain book left me feeling. The words roll off, but the essence, the true learning, remains.

I have long recognized that our minds are multi-faceted. It is no secret that the "thinking" part of the brain, a tiny region in the left hemisphere known as Broca's Region, is responsible for linking language to experience. This function accounts for only 5 percent of our total brain capacity. Linguistic thinking is obviously functional and necessary, even in its inherent limitations. And what are those limitations?

A primary limitation of the thinking mind is its relentless drive to create continuity, and thus meaning, by linking one thought logically to the next. The result of this process is called "linear logic." This logic attempts to create a mental chain of cause-and-effect relationships, and is often associated with what we would also call left brain functioning—the greater activity of the left hemisphere of the brain in this particular mode. To see this linking function in action, just listen in on any conversation. Notice how each contribution to the conversation is directly triggered by what was just said by the other person. And the listener's response continues to contribute to this chain of logical references. Of course this is all perfectly logical and natural from the verbal mind's perspective, so what is the big deal in even noticing it?

In order to answer that question, we will need to examine thought itself. A thought arrives wrapped up in a word or phrase. More accurately, the thought first arrives as a mental image or picture to which we automatically ascribe meaning with some past-referenced word, phrase, or image. Psychologists agree that all thoughts arrive first as images. The verbal label we choose usually has an agreed-upon meaning for ourselves and those we interact with. Many of our jokes and humorous moments come when the assumption of shared meaning is derailed momentarily, reminding us how fragile our sense of agreed meaning can be.

A thought, word, or meaning represents the ability of the mind to reduce the totality of experience to a single minute part of the whole with only one ascribed meaning. Thought, then, is a reducing exercise. We are reducing a full and complete moment of pure and unadulterated experience to a pre-conditioned slice of reality that essentially, leaves us existentially impoverished, whether we know it or not. Part of us knows that by focusing our minds on only one pre-conditioned perception to the exclusion of all other possibilities, we are limiting ourselves to a "thought-made image" of ourselves, which, being partial and conditional on past experience only, cannot be absolutely true. As this chronic mental impoverishment is inherently uncomfortable, unconsciously reminding us of our existential loneliness, we rush to the next word, phrase, or meaning to keep alive the stream of consciousness we like to think is so very real. The compulsion to distract ourselves with thinking is evident in the constant chatter many of us engage in today through our technologies. You could say we are all "thought addicted" and adding just one more thought keeps us from the existential pain lurking in the silence. This is normal to most of us most of the time.

A person who has mastered an expanded state of awareness and transcended the limits of linear time–based thinking would call this "normal" process "blindness." The thinking mind is like the blind man's white cane, trying to determine direction and meaning one tap at a time, with no idea where it's actually headed.

The thinking mind creates a chain of cause-and-effect associations based on the hope that this chain has meaning and leads somewhere. Honestly now, are chains usually associated with liberation or bondage?

But when a chain of thoughts leads to a more sophisticated or global insight, an "a-ha" moment, we typically throw off the prior chain and its contents to embrace the greater truth that has been revealed. We have arrived at a new level of understanding. Once a destination is reached, the map is redundant. Like I said, you recall the essence of the great books you have read, but not necessarily the chains of reasoning that delivered that essence.

I can't go on here without quoting the modern spiritual teacher Eckhart Tolle's take on words and ideas:

> The Truth is far more all-encompassing than the mind could ever comprehend. No thought can encapsulate the Truth. At best, it can point to it. For example, it can say: "All things are intrinsically one (The Pearl of Great Price)." That is a pointer, not an explanation. Understanding these words means feeling deep within you the Truth to which they point.[1]

It appears that logical thinking is only a vehicle, not the destination of our full potential. There is a part of the brain/mind that is less attached to linear thinking. Some associate this less constrained function to the right hemisphere of the brain, generally regarded as more *yin* or feminine in its orientation, implying openness and receptivity rather than action and movement. This is the side of the brain where the poet, musician, and artist operate from when in their creative mode.

It is from the "whole brain" state, when both hemispheres are equally active, that we often make novel connections and intuitive creative associations. This is when your mind functions beyond the limits of language,

....
1. Eckhart Tolle, *Stillness Speaks* (Novato, CA: New World Library, 2003).

conditioned "meaning," and time-based trajectories of logic. This is where you experience the "essence"; an inner place of just "knowing." The typical Western-educated mind has become particularly imbalanced in its ability to operate from both hemispheres equally. Having learned to shut down the seemingly illogical messages that leak over from our intuitive mind, we have become biased toward a strictly material and instrumental orientation to life. We have become doubtful and mistrusting of ourselves as we hide in dark closets of limited rationality. It is no wonder that many feel humanity is lost and can't find the way home.

The good news is that as soon as we recognize trends within ourselves that are not producing desired effects, we can change our minds! In fact, the recognition of our limits alone indicates that an expansion has already begun. The part that sees this and desires to think and be different is beyond the mind as we generally think of it. This part of us is more accurately referred to as the "Will," and is actually in the driver's seat of all our mental functions. The Will could be associated with inner purpose or motivation. The Will operates from a higher vantage point than intelligence alone. Today, however, many of our Wills are asleep at the wheel or held hostage to the ego; a temporary identity we made up (more on that soon). I suspect that your Will may be stirring; otherwise you would not have been drawn to this book!

The expectation of a typical reader of books like this one is often to find the "right information" to unlock deeper understanding and ultimately, hopefully, peace of mind. Let me reassure you here and now that there is nothing of any value you could read here or anywhere else that is not already somewhere in your own mind. I cannot tell you anything you don't already know, at least unconsciously. All I can hope to do is remind you and point you in a direction where you will discover the unlimited well of wisdom within that is yours by virtue of your being alive.

To glean the most from your reading, become aware of your own pre-conditioned reactions to what you read. Watch yourself as you read. Be aware that your conditioned responses are not coming from who you truly are! They are simply the comfortable pathways of perception that so far have brought you to this point in life's journey, but in no way dictate where you can go from here. To enter onto a new path, you may need to abandon the familiar but limited path you have been on. This takes no small degree of courage, and maybe a growing sense of "there *has* to be something better than what I am experiencing of life so far . . ."

This is how I encourage you to read this book: Be an "open book" yourself. I decided to write this book around an outline originally created as a presentation I prepared some time ago for an online class. The class went well, but I realized that the material was only scratching the surface of what may be critical to the full appreciation and practical use of what was being offered.

Because I am convinced that the intuitive part of the mind operates in a much less limited quantum realm, and is thus not limited by ordinary time and space, I am confident that we are indeed "connecting," even in *this moment*, through entertaining these non-linear ideas and possibilities. Yes, despite the seeming solidity of bodies and the apparent uniqueness of individuals, on the level of this quantum mind, we are already and always One! Ideas are our common property and are freely available to all who desire them. Ideas of liberation are your birthright. They are a gift from your Creator when you are ready to accept them.

A simple model of the structures of the mind may be helpful here as the mind is the only level where true and lasting change can be made. Consider an iceberg peeking above the ocean surface. The visible top of the iceberg could represent the thinking mind, which is also the domain of the ego—all the accumulated thoughts and images we hold about who we think we are. The surface of the ocean only reflects back to us an image of our limited selves while obscuring the view below, where the greater part of our being rests below our awareness. The first thin layer of ice below the surface could represent the subconscious mind, where we have stuffed our fears, phobias, and inner conflicts out of sight but not very far away. The subconscious mind often dictates our automatic responses according to the conditioning held there.

Below this, and making up 90 percent of our total mind, is the large and complex superconscious mind. This is the part of the mind that not only automatically regulates all of the gazillion physical processes and events in our bodies that go on each second, but is also the rich repository of the accumulated human wisdom and knowledge handed to us by past generations. Even more expansive, the superconscious mind shares the same ocean of unlimited Universal knowledge and total awareness through its connection with all other minds and the Source of the ocean itself. This is the ocean of "Big Mind" that connects us all and truly makes us one. As each separate iceberg eventually completes its life cycle and melts, the distinction between the individual and the whole is gone. Ice is only water, after all, in a different vibrational state.

My advice, therefore, on how to get the most out of this book is this: Read it like you would any other book, but pay attention when something you read triggers even an ever-so-slight inner recognition, which may show up as the thought "I know that, I've always known that, I just never heard it said this way before. And . . . it just *feels* right." This is your expanded superconscious mind inviting you to come over where the weather is always fine and swim in its limitless ocean of potential and creativity. So relish the feeling. Put the book down and enjoy the feeling the ideas offer. It is a sense of connecting and expanding into a deeper level with a part of yourself that maybe you forgot about or pushed aside. The feeling of peaceful expansion is closer to the real *you* than any thought or concept could ever hope to be.

Some would call this inner place of expanded awareness "Spirit" or "Soul" or "Higher Self." Again, these are just concepts the logical mind uses for the sake of discussion. Equally, recognize when what you read may bring up resistance or challenge an assumption you have held dearly. Avoid analyzing; just observe. Ascribing conceptual meaning through compulsive naming may also be a way our ego (false self) defends itself against dissolving. As we will discover, this "voice in your head" that offers an endless stream of thoughts and impressions is in fact only a set of pre-recorded tape loops that you tolerate in the absence of the full knowledge of your True Self. The Soul itself has no need to attach meaning or a concept to itself. Why would what is without limits choose to limit itself?

If you read this book in this manner, you will mine the gold that you were meant to discover. The gold is in you already! Think of any book as a "mind mirror" that will show you only yourself. If you read it for "logic" and linear meaning only, you may get something out of it, but in the end you will put the book down and anticipate the next one, which might, if you're lucky, have the "right" information for you.

It is, after all, everyone's destiny to awaken to reality. This book represents a collage of ideas drawn from various notes and references. As I have chosen to write more from a "stream of consciousness" place rather than creating yet another linear road-map to happiness, you will see some repetition of key ideas as you read. I am confident that you will recognize the content herein as a "carrier" for deeper nuances of meaning best described as "feeling." I offer this repetition as a learning aid, as the rational mind, in its deep conditioning, benefits from frequent reminders of the truth it typically denies simply by thinking.

Thank you for your devotion to truth. I see you as you truly are: an extension of the same Divine Being I am. I celebrate our life as the One True Creation. Not limited by history or hopes of a future time, I join with you in love and Gratitude now . . . which is forever.

The first published book I wrote is called *Navigating the Collapse of Time: A Peaceful Path Through the End of Illusions*.[2] Like this book, that book was first put together as a presentation, in this case on the topic of 2012 and the Great Shift of the Ages. The challenge in writing that book was how to limit such a vast subject to a little over two hundred pages. It was my hope that the brief overview of subjects presented there would whet readers' appetites for further self-study and reflection.

A main theme of that book and this one is the philosophical point of view called *non-duality*. Non-duality represents a return to the perspective of "wholeness" upon the dissolving of false and thus illusory distinctions based on a premise of duality or separation. You could say coming to a non-dual understanding is a critical step in the process of transcending linear thought altogether. By this, I do not mean that we will at some point just stop thinking (although this is possible . . . I think!). I would prefer to say that having a non-dual perspective still leaves us free to think, but with less and less attachment to and investment in our thinking. As we step into the more peaceful

....

2. Red Wheel/Weiser & Conari Press, 2011.

states of non-dual perception, thinking remains practical for negotiating the needs of the moment although it no longer dictates our identity, thus limiting us to a little "thought-made" self, or ego.

With this book, I intend to offer some "meat and potatoes" ideas for the serious awakener. I am using this term in place of seeker. To think of oneself as a seeker implies that there is something outside yourself you must find, like a lost object, in order to become whole, complete, or spiritual. Most seekers also feel the "answer" will come from outside themselves at some future time. We live in hope, not realizing that hope eliminates the present moment of any potential for us to realize ultimate truth and awaken now. This is a favorite ego game—a "carrot on a stick" attempt to keep us forever unhappy with who and what we are right now (which, by the way, is already perfect and complete). There you go—your first non-dual thought!

By "perfect and complete" I refer to your true essence, which is Spirit. Spirit was, is, and will always be perfect and complete just as it was created. I do not refer to the thought-made self or ego as perfect or complete. The ego, which is nothing other than a concept of separation, can never be complete. In its self-defeating fear and guilt-ridden belief, the ego is as far from perfection as a lie is from the truth. The good news, as we shall discover, is that the ego is only an illusion.

The paradox is that if we hadn't started out as seekers, we might not have realized the seeker is not needed. So it's all okay . . . another cosmic joke . . . a seemingly purposeless puzzling paradox, perchance?

In the Biblical stories of Jesus, He often lovingly referred to people as sheep. This was an interesting analogy. Sheep are not known for their individual intelligence, as far as I know. They tend to flock together, and they tend to need fences, at least while young. A fence lets the sheep know they are protected. Their limits provide a sense of safety in a threatening and unsure world.

Concepts are like our fences, especially as we dress them up in commonly held beliefs. But fences ultimately keep us from our freedom. Eventually, something within us stirs and we feel a deep unhappiness with the status quo. We begin to question our fences and wonder what lies beyond them. So let the concepts herein create for you a sense of security as far as that is needed. But please do not let them limit you. The destiny of this herd of sheep—humanity—is not to be sheared and barbecued—it is to be liberated. This is the destiny of all humanity, and life on this planet and Universe, for that matter. No matter what happens in the meantime, life must and will find a way to expand. Life is like light—it only knows infinite expansion given the removal of all blockages. I am 110 percent confident that you already know this on some level. Think of these ideas as steps on a ladder that will, with each step, grant you a broader and more expansive view, but will inevitably take you out of the hole of your separate existence altogether. Then you won't need a ladder. You will have become your

Self. Why do you think that all of us, despite appearances, aspire to happiness, to becoming productive and useful, to becoming free of limitations and free to expand creatively without limit? Could it be because in some dark corner of our minds there is a glimmer of memory of all these things and more as being our natural state? If we never knew perfection in the first place, we wouldn't know what to desire or feel we lack. Within every aspect of density and apparent separation, there remains a "spark" of Divine memory. For some this spark acts as an annoying reminder that "something's not right," and so we may unwittingly resent our own Divinity. We choose to call this feeling "Divine discontent." Ultimately, our discontent is what helps propel us over and away from our fences.

For some the spark of Divine memory is like a beacon on a dark and foggy night, providing a sense of direction in what otherwise appears as a meaningless and eternal darkness. You are the determiner of what your "spark" means to you, as you are the determiner of all your experiences. Give your spark the purpose of leading you home, and it will. Resist it, and it will remain, as this spark can not and never will be extinguished. If it could, then there is no Creation, and there is no you. When you are ready, your spark will appear as the inner knowing that you are "safe at home while dreaming of exile" (as stated in *A Course in Miracles*).

As you read this book, I encourage you to consider the hopeful words of T.S. Eliot: "We shall not cease from exploration, and the end of all our exploring will be to arrive where we started and know the place for the first time." May the perfection of who you already are awaken in you now.

ONE

Ending the Drama

Life is a dream—for some a nightmare.

A s noted, I am a student of A *Course in Miracles*, which I will refer to as *the Course*. Despite how it sounds, this is not a religious work at all. Spiritual, yes, but religious, no. What's the difference? Quite a lot, it turns out. Spirituality is natural, personal, and rooted in direct experience. There is no such thing as secondhand spirituality. No one else's spirituality can serve as substitute for your own. Spirituality, it can be said, represents a natural developmental stage in human growth—a birthright. As we go beyond ego and survival as our main orientation for life and begin to entertain greater possibilities beyond the limited life of the body, we will have experiences that validate this natural expansion into a greater reality. When and how these experiences happen is beyond our conscious control. It is inevitable, though, that every one of us will have a personal Spiritual Awakening sooner or later.

For some, the awakening can come from working with a specific practice or discipline. For others, it just seems to "land" out of nowhere.

Religion, on the other hand, grows out of the attempt to codify a deeply personal Divine connection into a structure that can be learned by others and maintained as a specific form over time. With this noble intention, spirituality is "cut down to size" to meet the limited needs of humans as perceived by other limited humans at that time. To think that a system of belief or code of behavior based on someone else's experience can in some way impart a spiritual benefit to another is like thinking that one person can breathe for another.

The difference between religion and spirituality is analogous to the difference between ego and Spirit. We are all bona-fide schizophrenics in this sense. We walk a fine line between our thought-made ego-self and our divinely appointed Spirit self. Which "self" is ascendant in the moment is easily determined by answering the question, "How happy am I?" Spirit is in joy constantly . . . limitless joy without any specific cause. You see, if our joy is caused by something, then the joy is always contingent on outside events and limited by uncertainty about what will happen when the cause for joy is gone. This is conditional joy, concealing a deep fear of loss of joy. Spirit experiences *un*conditional joy all the time—no exceptions. Ego vacillates between states of conditional happiness and abject misery that is unable to even imagine causeless joy. "Causeless joy," or joy without opposite, is another non-dual concept!

Most of us find ourselves wandering between these two states or modes of being in an awkward and unpredictable dance. Some days we dance pretty well; other days we seem to be stuck with two left feet. Until we fully awaken to our Spiritual Self and consistently remain in that state, we tend to stumble around, half-asleep. One critical thing we are generally unaware of before awakening is the "third element" of our being: the Will, which sits as the chooser between the True (Spirit) Self and ego. The Will is called the "choice maker" in the Course. Even when we are asleep to the Will, it's still operating—it's just asleep and hostage to the ego. The dormant Will tends to exclusively lean toward the apparent safety of our past conditioning and the conditioning of those around us.

Even when we do automatically react as we always have, there is a microsecond of choice before we do. This is the "gap" of silence between primary perception and thought. The gap of decision is so tiny in those who yet sleep that it is easily obscured by the steady stream of ego-babble we entertain as "our thoughts." Yet how we react to any situation *does* represent a choice, albeit automatic—a choice to remain as we have always assumed ourselves to be; a choice to stay in line with a mental image of ourselves that seems to work, for now. But sooner or later the self-image will fail, and we will be in the strange and uncomfortable position of having to make an entirely new choice without the support of any past reference. The Will has awoken. Our new choice will be determined with our sincere asking, "What is it that I truly want to experience now . . . conflict and pain, or love and peace?"

Real spiritual experiences always increase our joy. This is partly because true spiritual experiences always involve an element of greater inclusion, expansion, and connectedness. This is love in its real meaning, an ever-expanding and creative field of total inclusion with the accompanying collapse of perceptions of difference and separation. Love on this level requires no concepts or thoughts to sustain it. The ultimate reconnection is between *you* (what you think you are, as separate from your Source) and *your Source*. We say reconnecting because the connection has always been there. We have just lost sight of it.

Religion and religious sytems typically evolve in reaction to the awakening experiences of one person or a small group of people. For whatever reason, at some point in time a group of people felt it necessary to attempt to conceptualize a largely subjective and abstract experience into a concrete form, typically ending up encoded within "sacred" writings. Not to say this is "bad" or "evil"; the codifying of spirituality in the past represented for the most part a sincere desire to share the benefits of the spiritual life with a larger population—this particularly in past ages with limited communication systems and illiteracy across the board.

The idea of "educating the masses" with an imposed secondhand spirituality, however, contradicts a basic tenet held by most Eastern faiths, where "(only) when the student is ready, the teacher will appear." This edict recognizes a Divine timing to our spiritual awakening that cannot be rushed or prevented. When the student is *not* ready, laying a set of beliefs or behavioral codes on him will typically be perceived as an unrequested imposition on his freedom and sovereignty or will feed into his self-image (ego) of being religiously special. The entire Western missionary credo, a form of spiritual colonialism, was and is based in the arrogant assumption that "one size fits all" and "the prevailing patriarchy knows best" for everyone when it comes to spirituality. Spirituality is thus torn from the realm of the strictly personal and intimate to one of a culturally defined pre-packaged product.

History tells the story. Religion, a human invention, tends to separate people into "believers" and "non-believers," despite many creeds and injunctions that altruistically suggest otherwise. Upon truly awakening, many people naturally drift away from the spiritual kindergarten of religion. This is not to say that someone can't have a genuine spiritual experience within a religious context. Spirit is not limited by any time or circumstance at all! For some, a religious context may offer the ideal environment for their emerging spirituality. Sheep like fences, right? But religion itself does not guarantee a spiritual experience or connection. The arrogance of dominating hierarchies, of dogmatic separation and "holy wars", is a sure clue that the ego is in the mix, as only ego is invested in hierarchies that separate rather than join. You can inherit a religion like you can an accent or hair color, but your spirituality is entirely up to you!

There are many non-spiritual religious folks who by their beliefs and actions display anything but greater inclusion and connectedness. Sadly, many religions become happy havens for the ego and offer institutional support for propagating fear, intolerance, anger, and even war. If you doubt this last statement, have you seen the evening news lately?

It seems that as soon as we try to organize anything in our world, certain group dynamics arise spontaneously. The field of social psychology documents fairly predictable group behaviors. In the world as processed through the ego's filters, any human organization tends to gravitate to the establishment of hierarchies, or to something I like to call the "cheese principle." This principle suggests the following: In any human organization, the leadership (those who like to think they are the cream) rises to the top and solidifies. The resultant cheese then resists recirculation, and even as the milk sours, will hold its position at any cost.

Evolutionary psychologists have offered that the first politicians were also the first priests. After all, it was the priests who had the "connections" with the almighty or the forces of nature, and so could sway the Great Spirit to assure good hunting or crops, and to avoid the dangers of an uncertain future. Priests had the "hidden knowledge" of how to please or pay off the Gods with the most appropriate rituals and sacrifices. Religious leaders assumed some of the first class-based power distinctions in human cultures, along with hunters. As power in unawakened humans tends toward corruption and self-interest, many religious officials became subject to the "cheese principle" and were deeply invested in creating and maintaining ongoing power structures in their societies. Priest-politicians became among the first promoters of wars on other humans (more recently declaring "war" on nature, women, gays, the poor . . .) all "with God on our side" . . . a sad and divisive tradition based on asserting temporal power that continues to play out this day on Earth. It is likely quite confusing to our extra-terrestrial neighbors, who must see our great potential alongside our bizarre tribal behaviors as puzzlingly contradictory.

The political philosopher Karl Marx had a great degree of insight into the true function of religion in modern societies. Despite his demonization by the true believers in capitalism with their preferred interpretation of history, Marx was a deeply spiritual man. One of his great insights was in seeing how religions generally serve as the philosophical arm of the prevailing economic system of the day. It was Marx who declared religion as "the opiate of the people," lulling them into complacency and acceptance of rigorous male-dominated hierarchies, senseless wars, and inequality. "It's okay, folks, you'll get your reward in the afterlife! But if you screw up and don't 'play ball' in this one, you'll have hell to pay! Oh yeah, and don't forget you have to work real hard at a job you hate for low wages to get to heaven." The priests support the politicians and their corporate sponsors who in turn support the priests with lip service to "religious freedom." How cozy!

The separation of church and state in the Western world, a concept often credited to English philosopher John Locke (1632–1704), was one of the "great leaps forward" in the liberation of humanity. It is precisely this freedom that allows me to make statements like these without being burned at the stake. It is a sad and tragic commentary that dualistic religions (religions still caught in the trap of ego mind and its fixation on good *and* evil) have been the cause of so much pain and discord, each one believing they somehow represent "God's Will." The fact that there are 50,000 different denominations in the Christian world alone, each with their own interpretation of "God's word," should tell you something about human thought-based perception as a means of maintaining separation and egoic specialness. The only way this could make any sense is if somehow this dualistic "god" of religion was not the true God of Unconditional love, but instead the projection of collective ego tortured by its own inner divisions. If the conflicted ego is your god, then I suppose you would be justified in worshipping a god of fear who wages wars to punish "sinners" and "evildoers"—basically those who don't agree with our interpretation of truth and thus pose a threat.

I have touched on only one aspect of the insanity of the world here. No matter where you look in the man-made world of madness, you will find the same glaring inconsistencies, and the cause of much suffering and division in the commonly held thoughts, attitudes, and beliefs of many as held in our institutions and unquestioned historical patterns. If anything today challenges the deeply revered "myth of progress," I would say that the tenacious hold of pre-literate and dualistic religious dogmas on society proves that we are still, in many ways, in the clutch, if not the shadow, of the Dark Ages.

IS THE MOVIE OVER YET?

This brings us back to the question of "ending the drama." How do we solve the problems of this mess of a world on the brink of self-destruction and oblivion? I will not even consider offering political, economic, or philosophical solutions from the same level of mind that created the problem. Most "solutions" in the world today simply do not work because they are only addressing the effects of a deeper, hidden cause of our woes. As in our symptom-suppressing disease care system, Band-Aids can only cover up symptoms; they cannot address root causes. I'm just going to say it: Solutions for the problems of the world and your life do not lie in "fixing" anything, but rather in *recognizing the world has no more reality than a dream and is thus not real at all!*

This statement definitely strikes at the heart of the ego's thought system, which we grew up with and accept without question. The ego's version of you and the world, as convincing as it may be, is essentially limited to the realm of sensory input and conditioning from others who likewise are limited to a conditioned material orientation. Just because the majority of people around us think and feel the same way does make the consensus viewpoint right. The part of you that chafes at the notion that *there is no world* is the part that may unconsciously suspect it is true . . . and if it is true, then the whole house of cards built up by our belief in ourselves as separate and independent egos could come tumbling down. To this I say "Great!" That belief system is going to come down sooner or later anyway, as any structure started in time will end in time. The idea that time-based structures are by necessity temporary is a basic tenet of Buddhism, a largely non-dual thought system.

"Where does the suspicion that we live only in dreams exist?" you may ask. Remember that spark within? The fact that the world is an illusion is one of its key messages, and this realization is a crucial step in your awakening. I am happy to tell you that the illusion is not only "unreal" but also destined to evaporate back into the nothingness from which it arose. It is just a matter of time. How can I be so confident? It's simple, really. Any belief or thought system based on error must eventually implode, because errors have absolutely no foundation or reality in and of themselves. Only truth is true. Only what is true is real. All the rest is simply nothing—even an error that is held so deeply and dearly by the part of the mind invested in separation. What is this error? It is simply our belief in the possibility of separation, from our Source and hence from our True Self and each other. As we recover from all our illusions of separation, even the distinction between Source, Self, and others must yield to the Oneness, which has never changed, remaining as it always has been.

However, the mind begs to argue. One cannot maintain a dualistic perspective without the presence of the opposite point of view. This is not a criticism or judgment—it is simply an observation. Here is where the error of separation becomes a lie that we live by. Conditioned thought systems only appear solid because of the many complex falsehoods built to prop up the weakness of the original error. The ego loves complexity, because with more complexity comes more confusion and ultimately surrender to something we are convinced is beyond our grasp. Yet the ego, as a construct based on unreality, can only come to insane conclusions. As long as it operates, the ego is a master of smoke and mirrors used to distract from the simple, obvious truth that we remain One and that the separation it imagines is completely meaningless.

The ego's greatest fear is that once you awaken, you will realize (make real) the fact that you no longer need an ego. As a limited, self-contained, and self-perpetuating program, the ego has no single delete button, like a nasty computer virus. It is up to another part of the mind, the part that *is* real, to create and push that button often until the job is done and the virus is eliminated for good.

The way the "game" of life is constructed seems slanted toward the survival of the ego. After all, we made up the ego, and we are Divine co-creators. Anything we do, we do very well! The dualistic thought system is airtight inside its own operating system. In other words, "alternate" thought systems like that of non-duality make absolutely no sense within the ego's thought system, and are therefore easily discounted, if not arrogantly mocked and denigrated. This why hearing "the world is an illusion" can bring up anger and fear in some. This is also why it is not wise to attempt to convince anyone of anything against their will. Rather, the awakened one simply understands where the ego is coming from, and gives it no power whatsoever to shake the rock-solid foundation of Spirit's truth. We forgive, which means to overlook the impossible, and choose peace over conflict. I have always felt that if there is such a thing as Universal Truth, then it has to be very simple and accessible (and it is!). After all, most of us are essentially simple beings once we discard the ego's façade of false complexity. In fact, most humans on Earth today do not deal with the same level of complexity that plagues the technologically advanced but spiritually impoverished peoples of the civilized (read: "citified") world. As they have been for millennia, most people are simply involved in the day-to-day concerns of surviving and supporting their families and loved ones as best they can.

To say that the world of human ego-drama is not real flies in the face of our trust and confidence in our own senses. The modern scientific method is built on the foundation that what can be seen and measured is real; all the rest is not real (or suspiciously dubious at best!). This blind trust in our senses as the final arbiters of reality is flimsy at best and ludicrous at worst, especially when you consider how severely limited and thus unreliable our senses really are! The flat world and Earth-centered cosmos of the recent past were both firm beliefs based on the logic of the senses. It is our sensory perception of the separation of bodies in space that offers some of the strongest support to the ego's credo of separation as universal and irreversible. Yet do our senses really make sense at all?

An insect with different sensory apparatus exists in a completely different world. Which world is real—yours or the bumblebees'? To ascribe ultimate and exclusive meaning to a universe based on one species' sensory apparatus is tragically reductionist, and most of all reduces you and your creative, infinite mind to a lump of conditionally cultivated neural circuits.

Psychologists know that even sensory perception can be mediated by expectation and bias, as when witnesses often attest to differing accounts of the same event in court. If one criterion of true reality is that it must be consistent and changeless over time, then we could say that whatever is changeable does not qualify as essentially real. If something in our world can change with the flip of opinion or desire to see things differently, is anything we perceive in fact "real" at all? Optical illusions where two contrasting images trade places with each other depending on your point of view illustrate this fact. Only you can answer the question of what is truly "real," and only if and when you are ready to identify and challenge your own assumptions.

Once we understand that the horror flick of human drama is simply a movie based on our conditioned assumptions, we have the freedom to get up and leave the theater altogether.

WHAT IS REAL?

So if our senses and sense-made world is not "real," what is? Simply put, everything else as One energy field is . . . well, *almost* real. It is in fact the ineffable and ephemeral cause of that field of "All That Is" that *is* ultimately real. True reality transcends even this Universe of matter, time, and space. This "ultimate non-dual idea" requires a relinquishment of the need to give shape, form, or value to any conditional reality. As long as we appear to be here in our own movie, however, it seems pretty well impossible to do this. We can begin to move in the direction of true liberation by being willing to even entertain these thoughts. In a way, we must give up trying to make something out of nothing. We stop generating a thought-based identity and world when we realize we are doing so from a very limited state of awareness. Ultimately, we move from the concrete to the abstract as we expand our awareness beyond all sensory and cognitive limits. The movement toward individual expansion can be viewed as developmental and natural, as Humanist psychologists such as Erikson and Maslow have taught. Again, you cannot force development. It happens when it happens. But happen it will, because outside of time, it already has!

Let's talk about this word "reality" as we generally think of it. This is a term that can cause confusion unless we agree upon some contextual meaning. In most cases when we say "reality" we are referring to what we should call "conditional" or "personal" reality. In your reality, strawberry ice cream might be delicious, but in my reality it might make me sick! As far as we are usually concerned in our day-to-day existence, "our" reality is sufficient. There's plenty in my reality to keep me busy. And of course, I need to be careful that I respect your reality, too, for us to get along. We only come across difficulty when personal realities clash over, let's say, differences of perception or opinion. "What . . . did you bring strawberry ice cream home again?"

When we say "reality" in the context of spirituality and the prospects for human growth and even survival, we need to go up a notch and recognize an "ultimate" reality, or a one, shared, and inclusive reality. If we could all agree on a single shared reality, do you think we might have discovered a basis for world peace instead of petty and mindless conflict over whose illusion is superior?

This points to one of the many reasons I personally embrace the message of the Course, as it offers to the Western mind an invitation to enter into a dialogue that recognizes a common spiritual reality that connects us all, yet outside the traditional "conditional realities" of religion and limited human understanding. The Course represents a uniquely Western non-dual thought system.

One of the methods the Course offers for coming to terms with the insanity of the world is to think of it as no more real than a dream. In the sleeping dream state, no matter how crazy or improbable things are, the dream *is* our "reality" . . . until we wake up and shake off the dream, dismissing it as whimsical nonsense that did not really happen. No more pizza at midnight for me! Dream realities require us to remain asleep in order to maintain the semblance of continuity. I am reminded of how in the Bible, Adam was said to be placed in a deep sleep so Eve could happen, leading to all the trouble those two got into. Nowhere does it say he woke up! Are we missing an important clue here? The beginning and end of the story of this world is nothing more than a dream fable, like the movie in which the hero wakes up, much to his relief, at the end of an insane series of impossible circumstances.

Here's a question for you. What if, when we wake up in the morning from our "sleeping dream," we simply emerge into a more sophisticated "waking dream"? Would not this imply that the next step toward reality will involve, on some level, waking up from *this* dream? If we could wake up from our waking dream, would we not be able to look at our experience of the world and the body and its dreadful dramas with the same release and relief we experience when waking from a sleeping dream?

When you think about it, a hallmark of the sleeping dream is its crazy images, sporadic time sequencing, and unrealistic associations and distortions of familiar people, places, and things. How different is this from the waking dream except that we have told ourselves the waking dream is real? I'm not seeing many qualitative differences between the two varieties of dream states.

The great theorist of mind, Sigmund Freud, suggested that every image in a sleeping dream represents some aspect of the self. This concept was the basis of psychoanalysis and the idea that dreams provide the "royal road to the unconscious." When we consider that the experience of the waking dream is nothing but the result of internal neurological process that happen on the level of the mind despite the impression that the world appears as outside of us through projection, we come to the same conclusion. Every image in *this* dream is the projection of an inner self-image, as stated in the metaphysical precept, "All I ever experience is myself." As in lucid dreaming, awakening within the dream of oneself in the world has been called by the self-titled "stand-up philosopher" Timothy Freke as *lucid living*—knowing you are a character in your own dream but at the same time knowing that your true Self is awake and outside the dream.[3]

I find it interesting that in the context of the dream analogy the goal of many spiritual traditions, especially the more seasoned ones, is "awakening." The story goes that when his disciples asked the Buddha, "Who are you?" he simply replied, "I am awake!"

More recently, the theme of "dreams within a dream" was masterfully presented in the movie *Inception*. Movies

....

3. Timothy Freke, *Lucid Living* (Carlsbad, CA: Hay House, 2005).

have an uncanny way of reflecting the consciousness of their times. Are we on the threshold of a vast cultural awakening to the fact that our "tangible world out there" is no more than a projection of the state of our minds "in here"? If so, we may come to realize that before we can hope to change the world we must each take responsibility for changing our minds about the world.

Psychology is a field full of contradictions and differing viewpoints. It purports to understand the mind from the perspective of the mind that it is trying to understand— quite a challenge indeed! In its early days, psychology was disdainfully regarded by the more "serious" empirical sciences as soft—not to be taken seriously within the paradigm of strict research-based, statistically significant hard science. As a result, the academic world of psychology was swept up in the behaviorist movement in the 1950s in an attempt to legitimize itself in the judgment of the "big brother hard sciences" within academia.

Psychology researchers at this time wanted to be taken seriously and most likely also wanted to receive funding support equal to that of other disciplines. Thus, behaviorism literally attempted to reduce the entire human experience to what could be statistically measured and tested, according to the sacred cow of the scientific method. Subsequently, much of human intelligence and behavior was assumed to be on par with that of lab rats. The boys in the white coats tended to look at the rest of humanity as test subjects that needed to be guided and controlled by "those who know what is best for us" as proven by their lab rat experiments. This led to a lot of insane approaches to education and public health care, all "scientifically sound" but essentially crazy. The behaviorists, under the tutelage of their guru B.F. Skinner, envisioned a future society of a homogenized and pacified workforce building a sterile utopia all engineered and controlled by . . . guess who? Academic scientists and their corporate patrons, of course.

For the behaviorists, any quality or attribute that did not yield to observable and measurable data was simply crossed off the list of what was true or real—silly things like love, empathy, joy, forgiveness, and honesty. Who needs 'em? Let the soft-headed masses turn to religion, or better yet, let them watch TV!

Some examples of science run amok are the use of unproven vaccines on innocent school children, the introduction of toxic fluoride into the water supply, and the grand GMO experiment we are all unwillingly partic-ipating in today. At one time our science was what saved us from religious dogmatism, superstition, and blindness. Despite many advances and advantages offered by sci-ence, now we can honestly plead, "God save us from our science!"

Of course behaviorism fit hand in glove with the phar-maceutical industry's singular focus on the biochemical causes of illness and anti-social behavior. "A pill for every ill" replaced all kinds of ridiculous natural approaches to healing like applying kindness or compassion, or his-torically valid modalities like homeopathy, herbology, and naturopathy. Coupled with this was the politicized promise of our right to the "pursuit of happiness" through instant gratification offered by the growing material goods industry. The perfect society under a behaviorist model would have left us all a bunch of drooling lobotomized idiots perpetually plugged into the TV and never experiencing a pure moment of just being human. Do you think they may have succeeded, at least to a degree? You've got to give Big Pharma an "A" for effort.

Thankfully, a few free-thinking psychologists realized the dangers of the reductionist model as applied to humans, and "rediscovered" the value of love and compassion in the therapeutic environment. This was the birth of the Humanist movement in psychology, which opened the gates to even more expansive research and understanding which, for those early pioneers and their students, ultimately led all the way back to the understanding of Spirit as our essential nature. Humanists showed that the mind can not be reduced to a brain, but is much more free, adaptive, and creative than any conditioning alone could mold or limit.

The psychology of perception is an interesting blend of behaviorism and neuroscience. Researchers in this specialized field were focused on measurable results, eventually learning that our experiences of the outer world were primarily mediated and modulated by inner neurological processes involving specific brain structures, specialized cells, and neuro-chemicals. These researchers were beginning to understand that the world "out there" is truly all in our minds—something Buddhists had been saying for centuries.

If our perceptions of the world are dependent on neurological processes alone, then just how independently "real" or solid is the world out there? If altering brain chemistry can change our experience of the outer world, then which world is real? If the scenarios we perceive are continuously changing form and morphing before us as we ourselves change and adapt, how essentially "real" are our perceptions to begin with?

A major question still asked by brain/consciousness researchers is "How flies the arrow of causation?" Are our inner and outer experiences merely the result of brain chemistry and structures, as the pharmaceutical industry would prefer to believe, or does the mind independent of the physical brain provide causation, and thus somehow determine the brain's activity and all of physical life? This notion, though true, frightens many in the field because it begins to point toward a Creator—a "Great Mind" as the ultimate cause behind the Universe of matter. This is a little too close for comfort for the "new religion" of materialistic science to entertain.

The scientific world is still feeling the singes of the witch trials of not-so-long ago, when it endured the blind rage of paranoid religion. Science is not yet ready to cross the line into a metaphysical concept of reality, but ultimately it will. The pioneers who advanced the integration of science and metaphysics still consider themselves scientists, but they have begun to unlock the mysteries of Spirit, whether they call it that or not.

Of course, quantum physics has now provided a rationale for appreciating the unlimited nature of the mind. As

Einstein said, "The field is everything." In other words, all material form emerges temporarily into our awareness from a "field" of all potentiality. Later, researchers were able to demonstrate that it is our attention and expectation that literally collapses the energy held in this field into whatever it is we have chosen to experience—that we literally create our own reality by simply showing up and being there. No longer just a New Age platitude, co-creativity is rock-solid science.

QUANTUM LEAPING

I will not attempt to map the history and discoveries of the pioneers of quantum physics here. But there are three *very basic ideas* that merit mention for our purposes. No matter how far out these ideas may appear, they are among the most experimentally valid findings of twentieth-century science. In the last hundred years, no other branch of science has been as solidly backed by careful and exact research as has quantum physics. It is strange how we still haven't completely integrated these ideas as a culture, for their implications are profound and promising. Tragically, our current disease care system, which still looks at biology on a purely biochemical level, is the last holdout in the resistance to quantum science. Despite its glaring deficiencies and lethal so-called side effects, the "drugs and surgery" approach still seems paramount in the field of scientific medicine. When corporate profits dictate how we care for the sick and elderly, we witness a particularly cruel application of the ego's insane logic.

Quantum idea number one is the notion of indeterminacy. This is the idea that if you look at a subatomic particle (something that lies between matter and energy, of which all matter is composed) you can predict either its direction or position, but never both. You cannot predict its location based on its direction of motion, or vice versa. This proven fact challenges the whole notion of the "solidity" of matter. Because all matter is composed of energy in the form of moving subatomic particles, this principle suggests that nothing on the material plane is strictly limited to obeying physical "laws" alone. As everything we see is in constant flux with its surroundings, it is thus, as per our earlier discussion, not tangibly "real" in and of itself. There are simply too many factors influencing physical manifestation to place our faith in limited measurable associations alone. This realization can contribute to a sense of chaos and unpredictability, which is initially unsettling to the rational mind. However, the upside of this potentially disturbing idea is that we live in a Universe of all possibilities. Chaos and the potential for change, we discover, is a necessary prelude to creativity. The "field" that Einstein recognized as behind all phenomena is a dynamic ocean of pure potential waiting for an observer to pull the energy into material manifestation by the act of merely paying attention.

Idea number two follows from the first. It is the idea of "non-locality," which describes how, at finer levels of energy, events cannot be limited by the ordinary parameters of time or space. Subatomic particles communicate in pairs (the most basic "units" of duality, if you like) across vast distances of space-time *instantaneously*. Time and space are separation concepts that seem to operate in the 3D physical realm, but do not hold up when we consider subtler levels of matter and energy, such as subatomic particles and the energy of thought itself. Even the speed of light has a physical limit, but your thought is completely free to roam the Universe unhindered by any protests of your logical mind's belief in limitation. Non-locality infers that there are aspects of Creation—dimensions, if you like—where the "rules" of physicality simply do not apply. As Einstein observed, the position and trajectory of an object is simply relative to the motion of the surrounding space. The challenge to the rational mind is that none of the rules that provide us with a sense of security here in the physical world hold up absolutely, so can we really trust our senses? If you consider that humans are multi-dimensional and not simply limited physical beings, this concept further implies that there are aspects of you that are not limited by the body, time, or space. You as Spirit are free. You exercised your freedom when you chose the experience of separation, and you are equally free to choose to remember the knowledge of Oneness.

Key to the full appreciation of non-locality is the phenomenon of thought itself. The mind/brain complex is physically represented in the brain and nervous system. The brain, in its bicameral functioning with two distinct hemispheres, creates what physicists and researchers have called a *scalar wave* or place of *zero-point* energy. These terms describe what occurs when two equal but oppositely charged electromagnetic fields converge and overlap, like the measurable electromagnetic fields the brain generates. Even though the electromagnetic signature of the two hemispheric fields cancel each other out at the point of intersection (due to their opposite polarities), *something* has to occur in the space.

The pioneering researcher James Maxwell (1831–1879) theorized about these higher non-measurable ranges of energy, coining the phrase "hyper-spatial dimensions" to describe the intangible nature of these energies. Even without the backing of quantum science or modern measuring equipment, Maxwell presumed that there were dimensions of reality that were somehow linked to what could be measured, but far beyond any observable phenomena. Later, researcher Colonel Tom Beardon coined the term "scalar waves" to describe the energy that appears to create an opening into non-physical realms of energy.

If you consider that the two hemispheres of the brain biologically generate the fields required to create a scalar opening, we have a basis for grasping the non-local potential of the human mind to impress intention into these realms and operate non-locally. We now have at least a rudimentary grasp of how things like telepathy and distance healing can occur. Before these potentials can be unlocked, however, there needs to be a degree of acceptance and understanding on the part of the conscious mind, which would otherwise sabotage the subtler levels of mind-functioning with its own "logical" doubts and fears.

So, even though the body is limited to 3D density and the rules of Newtonian physics, the mind as a generator of non-local scalar waves is not similarly limited. Our minds are free of any limitation they may imagine in their current state of spiritual amnesia. Ask any survivor of a "near-death experience" and they will confirm that the mind is completely whole and functional without necessarily being rooted in the soil of the physical body.

The third proven quantum principle is known as the "observer effect." This is simply the idea that in order for non-local subatomic energy to manifest in space-time, a conscious observer must be present. Stated differently, an aspect of mind must be present and willing to have an experience in order for the experience to manifest. Here we have a scientific fact in support of mind as the cause of the brain, and not the other way around. This principle answers the question, "If a tree falls in the forest and nobody is there, does it make a sound?" The answer is that if there's nobody there, there's not even a forest, much less a sound. Consider that when a group of people are having a common experience such as watching a movie or listening to a lecture, they are all convinced they are having the same experience. Yet each one, depending on their angle of view, their expectations, and so on, are having completely unique and individualized experiences. Each one is observing a different story based on their own inner processing of the information. We are all only ever experiencing ourselves! No two experiences are the same, yet we agree we are enjoying them "together." Perhaps this is conditionally true, yet no one observer's experience is the same.

Grasping and accepting the observer effect as a "given" opens one up to a first glimpse of the true and perhaps unrealized power of the mind. When we observe a distant star over oceans of time and space, there is an instant exchange of photons between observer and star that literally changes the energetic makeup of both bodies. This exchange does not occur within the limits of the physical speed of light; otherwise, it would take light-years for the effect to take place. As the true exchange occurs in the higher octaves or dimensions of light not limited to Newtonian dynamics, we are witness to a truly non-local event.

Consider that this level of energy exchange occurs with every thought, and you may begin to appreciate how your mind literally "fills the universe" and is absolutely unbound and free in its potential. Here we begin to use the word *mind* not in the limited, personal sense of my mind or your mind, but in the classical sense of mind, heart, and Spirit being one and the same. This is our True Identity; though we may be convinced that the dream of separation and individuality somehow trumps reality, we continue to function on the level of creative or "big" mind, limited only by our belief that we are not that. The challenge is to simply do what we do all the time, but consciously.

Together these proven scientific principles help to punch holes in our conditioned assumptions about the nature of reality. One common element they point to—and again, this is only a very cursory look at these ideas—is the primacy of the mind. Returning to the mind as a level of cause is a critical phase in the spiritual awakening process. Quantum physics has helped fill the void left by the "learned ignorance" perpetrated by dualistic religions, including the religion of modern science, upon the Western mind. Spirit will reach us in whatever context we can accept. Eventually, all paths, all seven billion of them currently, lead home. No one is left out because of circumstance or historical disadvantage. After all, there really is only One of us here—even though it is still dreaming it is having different experiences at different times.

Considering these quantum ideas, the "dream" analogy begins to make even more sense. Just as the rules of time and space are flexible in the sleeping dream, we see how the rules of the waking dream are not that solid either! The psychologist Carl Jung, like Freud, was fascinated with dreams. In 1953, his interest in dreams led him to the study of a natural society from the jungles of Malaysia, the Senoi. This culture had a very interesting approach to the dream world. Each morning the tribal elders would convene (over coffee?) and share their dreams from the night before. Based on their interpretation of this "reality," they set about the day following the blueprint outlined in the dream state. In other words, for them, the sleeping dream was a more reliable picture of reality than the waking dream. And this way of living and being seemed to work just fine.

We put quantum principles to work every time we go to the movies. We visit outer space and sail the vast oceans of the past and future without a second thought. For two hours, we willingly suspend most of our rational faculties while we are swept away in fantastical images and sounds coming from the screen. Although part of our mind is still cognizant that we are at the movies, the greater part of our attention is hypnotically surrendered to the whim of Hollywood's latest manufactured fantasies and special effects. We physically, mentally, and emotionally respond to the events and stories as if they were literally happening to us. Perhaps they are, as the observer effect suggests. Is the world on the screen any different than the world in the theater of our own minds that we walk around in every day, behaving as if *that* movie is real? Pass the popcorn, please. We're getting to the good part.

It is undeniable that this world-movie is awash in drama. To regain our sanity, we need to bust the blocks inherent in the planetary blockbuster! Much of this psycho-thriller movie we call the "real world" is reflected and amplified to deafening levels by our drama-obsessed media and its penchant to spread the pain and angst of humanity's suffering far and wide. "We're just giving the people what they want," the media moguls whine. This is the logic of drug pushers. We are more connected to the sordid horror stories of this world than ever before. What could possibly be the benefit of keeping people locked in the insanity of the dream? What part of us is afraid to wake up from the spell and leave the theater altogether? I think you know.

We have seen in our inquiry so far that the drama of this life is literally experienced as an internal mental process inside each observer. This is very encouraging; if the "world is in our mind," are we not therefore in a position to change our minds about the world, and thus change the world itself? Mind = cause, world = effect. No exceptions.

We determine a thing's value by the purpose we ascribe to it. Social psychologists call this attribution theory. From this perspective, nothing means anything until we give it a meaning based on the perceived value it holds for us. So we must ask, "Where does all the drama get us, and what, if any, is its purpose?" The world outside us can only reflect either the ego or Spirit, as these are the only two identity-paths our minds can choose. The "choice maker" in you makes this decision in every moment, either consciously or by default, depending on whether the Will is dormant or awake. Those on auto-pilot seem to follow the same map over and over, and typically get to the same predictable destinations. Those whose Wills are awakening realize they can indeed choose what purpose they give their experience, and have the total freedom to choose differently.

In his groundbreaking work with plant intelligence, researcher Cleve Backster identified what he called "primary perception."[4] Initially known for his polygraph work with the CIA, Backster described an automatic biological response to the environment that occurs on an energetic and biochemical level when a plant comes into contact with an environmental stimulus. This innate intelligence is not limited to plants. In animals, including humans, this inherent biological intelligence is called "electro-physiological reactivity" or EPR. In humans, there is a measurable increase or decrease in electrical activity in response to either a supportive or stress-inducing stimuli. "Reactivity" is primary biological perception before meaning. Depending on our sensitivity and self-attunement, we might perceive these subtle nudges as attraction or repulsion to a food, substance, person, or situation, and then ascribe this reaction to intuition or gut feeling.

As humans equipped with a language-based consciousness, we automatically give our experiences meaning in order to "understand" what is happening to us and to determine a course of action based on whether we perceive stimuli as friend or foe. This is what makes humans "rational" rather than purely instinctual. In the ego's limited perception, however, we drag all past references of similar experiences into the moment, and cast a spell of conditioning upon our primary perception. This process extends up to the macro level in the form of what Deepak

....

4. Cleve Backster, *Primary Perception: Biocommunication with Plants, Living Foods, and Human Cells* (Anza, CA: White Rose Millennium Press, 2003).

Chopra calls "the hypnosis of social conditioning." Our perceptual apparatus not only reduces an experience's meaning to match a similar experience from the past, but also tends to cut us off from truly novel or creative interpretations and responses while creating the impression of apparent safety and continuity.

Does recovering our intuitive intelligence mean becoming more sensitive to our own primary perception? If so, we could learn to recognize our conditioned responses as the automatic mental reactions they are and our unconditioned body signals that operate from primary perception to be more indicative of the actual choices we have in each situation. This expanded field of choice can be most effectively achieved through desire (the Will) and the intentional cultivation of inner mental silence, which is a topic we'll explore soon.

Perhaps the best way to think of the dramas in our world is to consider what a huge distraction they are from the really good things in life—from a life we all claim to prefer. How much of our precious time do we give away to the meaningless dramas on our inner movie screens? Who is stopping us from getting up and leaving the theater when we realize the movie is a genuine turkey?

As we shall see, we can shift the experience and effect of our dramas by giving them a new purpose: that of awakening. In many cases, the inner frustration and the psychic toll of our dramas can propel us forward in our awakening process. We begin to find out who we truly are and what we truly want by eventually realizing what we *don't* want! When the insecurity of "not knowing" appears more appealing than the ongoing drama we find ourselves drowning in, things begin to move both within and consequently without us in support of that desire. The Divine hears the signal, and throws us a lifeline.

Ending the drama begins with our acceptance that the drama comes from us, and that we are never victims of the world we see, but only of our own thoughts. Owning this understanding is both humbling and empowering. Without this flip into responsible maturity, we can only count on more of the "same old same old." No worries here, though, as our ongoing suffering is only a facet of time, and time itself, as a mental construct, has no essential reality. We are only imprisoned by the bars of our limited thinking. As you read on and allow the thoughts herein to begin to dissolve some of your preconceptions, the prison bars will become transparent and inevitably disappear. After all, they were only thoughts to begin with.

TWO

Earth School

With all the chaos in our personal and public worlds, we might sometimes feel like getting off the bus *now*, even before it gets to where it's supposed to be going. Students of history quickly realize that no matter how modern and advanced we seem to be in this day of instant communication and technological wonders, the human drama of pain, suffering, and inequality drones on generationally in one form or another.

As mentioned earlier, the modern media has been a mixed blessing in this sense. Yes, the media does bring us together as a community, nation, and world in many productive ways. Consistent within duality, the media also disconnects us in many unproductive ways. For example, in the pre-industrial era, when there was human tragedy, the extended family and immediate community were directly affected. Those close to the drama had the option to do something about it. Perhaps neighbors stopped by to offer condolences or assistance. The burden of suffering was carried together, and the blessings of communal support helped individuals move on.

Now, when there is a local tragedy, it is quickly splashed over national media. It becomes everyone's emotional experience. That's a whole lot of reactionary energy funneled into the collective consciousness field without any direct way of offering consolation or assistance, other than writing a check, I suppose. The virtual community is so vast and interconnected that we can only watch in horror and hope for the best for the victims, while praying the same thing never happens to us or those we love. When we hear about a tragic event hundreds or thousands of miles away, what does it do to our energy? Do we feel empowered or helpless? Did it really make any difference to those directly affected to have their story of suffering blared around the world as entertainment for the masses? What of any value can come from this artificial amplification of pain? Only ego is served by the perception of pain and suffering. And ego has an agenda—one that is hopelessly self-defeating. The ego is programmed to survive as a thought-entity at all costs by maintaining a limited sense of self as vulnerable and deserving of suffering. The agenda is simply "Stay asleep!" I am happily anticipating the day when the public media serves the truth and is used to uplift rather than enslave.

I find it curious that many people I speak to feel the world is getting worse and worse, but statistically, the amount of deaths from warfare and violence are on the decline, as are crime rates in general. We are better fed, better educated, and living longer these days. Again, I think we can fairly acknowledge the media as a means of social control. Fearful people are much less likely to rock the boat by challenging the status quo. They are more likely to attempt to protect what little they think they have. Is this not slave mentality?

This brings me back to a fundamental question we need to ask about anything we experience in this world. What is the purpose of our experience? And who benefits? Does the world, including nature and culture, have a reason to exist, or are we simply caught on a Mobius strip of cruel fate as we dance to the random tune of the Universe as it winds down in entropy? This was the sad conclusion of the early existentialist movement, circa 1900 to the 1930s. In their understandable rejection of religious dogma in light of new scientific knowledge, the existentialists inadvertently threw out the baby of natural spirituality along with the bathwater of religion. This is the sad legacy of both atheistic materialism and modern dualistic religion. Both have served to obscure the knowledge of our true nature and potential.

By misrepresenting the Divine through their own limited and anthropomorphic projections, human dualistic religions turned those who were awakening to new vistas of human potential through education and science away from a truly integrated and natural spirituality. As antithetical examples of the espoused Gospel of Love and Forgiveness, and by their insistence on clinging to outdated and senseless dogma, institutionalized religions have lost practically all credibility with the free-thinking person in the emerging scientific age.

Unfortunately, when you toss out spirituality, you seriously limit yourself to the rational, linear mind as your default roadmap of existence. And reliance on this tiny, insufficient map alone only serves to deepen the inner anguish of separation. Many early existentialists, and the nihilists and anarchists that followed, ended up following a path of self-destruction and despair when they saw no way out of the ennui of their own disconnection and spiritual impoverishment.

The legacy of a de-spiritualized culture is that suicide is one of the top killers, though it is largely unrecognized in its many forms. The obvious suicides—the ones who leave notes or tell someone that they intend to kill themselves—are only a small proportion of those who have simply given up on life. How many of us merely put in our time with needless pursuits, endless chatter about nothing, and mindless media mush to avoid having to be alone with our thoughts of separation, pain, and suffering? A modern mind blinded to its Divine connection is in a sad and lonely place, albeit of its own design.

Other and less obvious ways that self-destructive thoughts and beliefs manifest include self-neglect through poor nutrition and lifestyle choices, enduring abusive relationships, working at jobs that offer no rewards beyond a paycheck, and adopting extremely negative attitudes toward others. Unloving behavior toward others and thus ourselves is epidemic in the post-industrial world, and it all stems from the same illusion: that we are somehow cut off from our Source, from love, and are undeserving of anything better than our appointed "lot in life" as determined by the prevailing economic culture. The unspoken rules we live by are nothing more than persistent beliefs— erroneous, but mutually held and culturally supported and replicated. Even New Age spirituality can be misleading if it only emphasizes bliss, love, and light. Without the experience that has been called the "dark night of the Soul," we cannot make room within our psyche for anything new. I beg to differ with the phrase, however, as the Soul, if Divine, knows nothing of darkness. A more accurate description of this experience of "hitting bottom" would be called the "dark night of the ego," as only ego knows of suffering.

Sooner or later we all must face the fact that the world is fundamentally insane and meaningless. Seeing this clearly is a good sign that you are actually 'going sane.' Despite the challenge to our own conditioning, this understanding is critical to our inevitable liberation from suffering. If you are at the point in your awakening when you suspect this may be true, I congratulate you and remind you that you will eventually understand the undeniable and liberating fact that the world is not only insane, but at root *is* an illusion and not real at all. After you get over that shock, the relief you feel will be reason to celebrate, and even laugh at how gravely serious you thought it all was.

Understanding the meaninglessness of the world and our own thoughts about it must come before we can ever hope to transcend the inner illusions that support our own and the world's suffering. Another way of stating this is to say that we must come face-to-face with the limits of our thought-made self, the ego, and see it clearly for what it is. Only then can we see our way of thinking and being from a part of ourselves merely obscured by this façade, but which is in no way affected at all. By dis-identifying with our pain and looking at it from a neutral place, we begin tearing away from the false self, which must ultimately reveal to us what was always there—a real Self, which is still and always One with All That Truly Is. This is a process as natural as new life emerging from a dormant seed.

The turning point in anyone's life can be triggered by any number of events . . . the unexpected death of a loved one, the loss of a home or job, or an illness. It is ironic that through what seem like our greatest losses, we often find our greatest gains. The Course came about after a frustrated medical administrator hit bottom over the chronic bickering and ineffectiveness of the board she had to deal with on a daily basis. When she and a colleague agreed, "There simply *has* to be a better way," miraculous things started happening.

You could fairly say that the world as we see it now (in 2014) is hitting bottom in numerous ways: ecologically, economically, politically, and in the areas of health care, education, and the legal system . . . in practically every arena. Is this bad news? For those still solely invested in dreams, yes. All dysfunctional relationships—personal, public, and political—have this one element in common: they are ruled by the ego, which itself is ruled by fear. And the ego's greatest fear is that you will find out that it is an illusion. Much like the realization that Santa Claus doesn't really exist, there comes a time when we are willing to accept "I've been duped!"

However, the dissolving of these dysfunctional ego-based systems is nothing but good news to your True Identity, no matter how this dissolution looks on the outside. The systemic insanity of the world being exposed now is giving way to new ways of being based on equality, dignity, and respect for all life. The old must be exposed and released for the new to take root, just as the soil must be turned over and exposed before the next planting.

The model provided by Chaos Theory shows that chaotic events and systems eventually yield to a greater level of organization. Within the duality of the "dream" of separation, you could say that chaos is a necessary prelude to greater levels of harmony and creativity. Although the ego mind craves continuity and is upset by incongruous events, it is in times of uncertainty that we can open ourselves to novel ways of thinking and being as we choose to creatively adapt rather than merely react to new situations.

If this spin on what is wrong with your world makes any sense to you, then I would say you have already decided, on some level, that "there has to be a better way." The inner optimism of life itself has broken through the limits of the mind in acceptance, or better still, the memory that "light is more powerful than darkness." The Will has awakened, and the inner "choice maker," your True Self, is back in the saddle!

Although the conceptual mind is of our own making, the Will comes from something else. The Will is your Divine spark, the part of you that never left your Source. It is the driving force that "keeps you in the game" despite your suffering or reluctance to remain. Every living thing carries this energy. As we fell asleep into the dream of separation, the spark was hidden under blankets of guilt, fear, pain, and suffering. Yet it remains the "most real" part of you! The spark of Divine Will in you is being activated by the ideas in this book, as they come from the same will in me—the Will to awaken to reality.

When the spark becomes a flame of full remembrance in all of us, we will know how to co-create the world we all truly want: a world of peace, harmony, and prosperity for all and on all levels. You could think of the "choice maker" within as the personification of your own spark— the evidence that the spark can affect your decisions and manifest through you. From a metaphysical perspective, your spark is evidence of a Divine Will, and the awakened choice maker is now capable of operating from identification with the Created One or one and only original Creation, which is us. The Will takes form as the life within. You who were once only the "Son of man" have become a "Son of God." (Apologies to all you "Daughters of God" . . . the Divine does not see any dualistic differences such as male or female. Feel free to use whatever terms you wish in regard to your Divine Self. God herself doesn't mind either way).

The Will is much more than a personal quality. We equate the power of the Will with the power of love—love being the manifestation of Divine Will. In other words, there is no division between "my" Will, "your" Will, or "God's" Will. One Will unites us all. Reality is One Love. The Will of love does not demand expression as one form over another; rather, it establishes a higher purpose for expressing ourselves as we will. The expression of the Divine Will is not limited to any behavioral code. It is equally present in the announcement of a grand social movement based on generosity and equality as it is in the gentle smile of a stranger passing by. It is the "Will to unite" in place of the desire to separate or isolate. The Will within you desires nothing other than to return to the full knowledge of reality and the fact that in truth, the separation at the root of our suffering is nothing other than a bad dream. Even as we sleep, the Divine Will is conspiring to awaken us all.

It is when we change the lens of our camera on the world in accordance with liberating ideas that we begin to see opportunity, where before was only bleak despair. A new rediscovered light is now seeing through our eyes. We have given the world a new purpose, and in this purpose (which is to awaken us to the truth of our Self) it shines.

This is why I like to think of existing in this world as being enrolled in "Earth School." If we are *not* here to learn what is truly valuable and enduring (real!), what's the point? To stoically endure suffering? Get rich and die? Accumulate the most toys before we do?

Earth School is graduate school for Souls dreaming this Universe. In this school, you cannot fail, but you may need to repeat some grades. We all graduate eventually—that is a given. The only choice we have is how long we want to suffer by not recognizing our "lessons" as opportunities to awaken. There is a proven timeless method to moving to the head of the class and graduating sooner. It is called true forgiveness and we'll say more about it soon.

THREE

Metaphysical Creation Story

We get into Earth School by deciding to awaken and go home to our Source. Until then, we are simply accumulating experience in the "prep school" of suffering. It turns out that Earth School is an excellent place in which to wake up. Otherwise, just hanging out on "psycho planet" can be unbearable. Either way, we are all here to learn the same thing: that our belief in our separation from Source and each other is only a dream from which we can and will awaken. We are here to accept the correction given by Spirit for all the false ideas we took on along with the dream of separation. To better appreciate how we are all on the same learning path by virtue of being here, it is helpful to provide some metaphysical background. You don't have to subscribe to the views I am presenting. I do, though, have an inner confidence that the part of you that knows all of this already, your inner spark, will recognize these ideas, and they may not seem entirely foreign to you. The following is gleaned from my ongoing study of the Course. And it *feels* right!

Before the Universe there was Creator, Prime Source, All That Is, Big Daddy in the Sky . . . whatever. This Being has no attachment to what we call it, as it transcends any description or sense of separate identity. That is why it best not get into conversation about the meaning of God in polite company, as no one seems to agree on what this "it" is! This is because *all* concepts fall short of what we are trying to describe—it is like trying to describe the qualities of an empty space. True spiritual adepts never try to describe Creator, as they have first-hand experience of the indescribable abstract nature of God and know discussion is meaningless and usually misleading. The ego, on the other hand, is highly invested in the "correct interpretation" of these things, knowing that its insistence on "being right" is another guarantee that we stay in separation and suffering. "Being right" automatically makes somebody wrong, and creates a false hierarchy in denial of our absolute equality as we are all created. All wars start with this insanity at their root.

Even physicists have thrown up their hands in trying to describe what was before the Big Bang, other than concluding that whatever it was/is, it is best described as an idea. So let's agree there was *something* there before the material Universe. Let's optimistically call it the idea of perfection—of perfect love. The Course is unique in that it makes a clear distinction between the Creator and the original Creation as us in our original state of perfect

Oneness, yet somehow distinct from Creator. You could say we are an extension of Creator as much as a child is an extension of their mother and father. Thus we co-existed alongside and as a part of Creator before the Universe. Within this unlimited shared field of all possibilities, inevitably the sub-idea or possibility of separation arose in the mind of the Creation (us): "What is it like *outside* of everything?" Nutty idea, right? Actually, the Course refers to this thought as a "crazy, mad idea." No wonder the world is insane. It is based on an insane premise.

Nonetheless, the idea, coming from where it did, carried weight. We as a collective spiritual entity *are the "only begotten Son of God."* Jesus tried to tell us this two thousand years ago, but under the spell of our own separation, we wanted a special hero to do the work for us and specifically to deal with the political oppression of the day. In our short-sightedness we seriously underestimated Jesus' true purpose. We undervalued His greatest gift of unconditional forgiveness. Maybe humanity of two thousand years ago wasn't ready to hear this. With the stakes even higher today, can we afford to ignore the message any longer?

This causal relationship: God (Creator) > Us (the First Creation) > the Universe (our mis-creation) addresses a big question that has been a major stumbling block to many people's acceptance of the concept of a Creator at all. Dualistic human religions teach that God created the world and that humanity came along later. Any rational person looking at the world with all its glaring contradictions, pain, and suffering can only conclude from this version of the Creation story that this God must be some kind of sicko to make a world like this. So they give up on God altogether. Now then, who does this whole idea serve? The correct answer is . . . ding! The ego!

It is much easier for me to accept that God created us as an extension of Himself, which is another way of saying love gave birth to love. Then we, in our impetuous curiosity and impulsive need to exercise our God-given right as a co-creator, took the power of Creation and in one little gaseous brain emission (referred to as "passing wind" in polite company) asked, "What would it be like to experience *more* than everything?" Being without fear of any kind and knowing the end of our fantasy from its inception, Creator in effect said, "Do you really want that? Go ahead and check it out." This was the conceptual force or "big idea" behind the Big Bang. We learned early on that if you whine hard enough, you may get what you want. But what you want may not be in your best interest!

The All That Is, perhaps a bit stunned at first at the audacity of the idea of separation, had/has every confidence in His own Creation to get over it and return to sanity. Judgment or resistance of any kind was/is not in the Divine Creator's vocabulary. We seemed to successfully project an aspect of ourselves outside of the totality of Oneness at the moment of the Big Bang. This aspect was of the same Light as the All That Is, yet, in its experience, believed it truly separated from All That Is. As we believed that we fell into the density of physicality, beginning as Light and eventually crystallizing as matter. Our sense that we had accomplished the desired separation appeared to be confirmed by our experience.

Now you might think the Light was happy in this state, as if setting off on a grand adventure. However, this was not the case. Rather, the Light realized that in its whimsical desire to experience separation, it was in fact lost and apparently cut off from its Source. We ultimately felt terrified and abandoned in this unknown wilderness of matter, space, and gravity. In our panicked state, we assumed that somehow we must have destroyed if not seriously damaged the Oneness we had come from in order to wind up here in this Universe of separation. We believed in our own terrible power to mis-create. This realization was horrific, like playing with a gun and finding out too late that it's loaded. The guilt that followed was an even deeper feeling of pain and despair. This is the existential guilt we all carry as an imprint from the original experience of separation. The Course refers to the belief in this separation, which as we'll see was simply an error in perception, as the "one problem" we are all here to solve. The crux of this story is the realization of the impossibility of separation at all. As a matter of fact, all of our experience of the Universe is only happening on the level of the creative mind that desired it, and is best described as a dream. A separate Universe full of separate beings, each having their own experience, is a projection of the "split" in our mind as we chose to know separation. It is our collective movie playing in the theater of a vast and powerful imagination. Too bad we were not aware that the Universe and the guilty suffering we accepted was all happening in a dream! The Big Bang was more accurately the Big Oops resulting in the Big Snooze.

The dread of thinking we split and tore the perfection we had once called home started a downward cascade of fear and self-blame, wherein the Light felt that its only recourse was to go all the way with this mad desire and take the experience to its conclusion. The ego, our substitute invented self, was completely conceived within the desire to justify to ourselves the experience of separation. Once in the driver's seat, the ego propels the insanity forward, preferring dreams of distraction over waking to the truth of its own illusory nature. This story as just described undermines everything the ego has taught us about our own nature and more importantly the nature of our Creator. Think of the image of an unconditionally loving parent watching a child asleep, safe in his bed. The child stirs, indicating he may be having a bad dream. The parent knows the child is perfectly safe at home despite his dream, and so chooses not to disturb the child until the nap is over. Sooner or later, the parent may lovingly whisper in the child's ear, "You've slept long enough, it is time to wake up. I have some wonderful things for us to do together and I know you're going to love it!"

This life is naught but a series of images being played out on the screen of our collective mind. And we here in Earth School are still part of that dream. Did I hear the bell ring? Is it time to go outside and play? Or is time to pack up our books and go home?

If we were to completely subscribe to our current sci-entific myth of Creation (that the Universe created itself by some mysterious "accident"), we might find ourselves arriving at the grim conclusion that we are all alone in the Universe and that all we have to look forward to is our own oblivion (as de-spiritualized empirical science would have us conclude). But, as in all really good stories, there's a "catch" that turns the whole plot around at just the per-fect time to rescue our hero.

The story of separation from Source is indeed a sad and frightening tale—*if it were true!* Once we ask the question (perhaps the first meaningful question we ever ask) "Is it possible that anything could exist outside of everything?" we get a first glimpse at the fascinating possibility that the Universe, in all its apparent vastness and complexity, didn't really happen at all in reality, but only in our vivid imagination.

In fact, the Big Bang, if anything, was no more than in instantaneous flash of light, like a flash camera going off in a room, which retracted back to its source the split second it was projected, just because of its inherent impermanence and thus impossibility as a sustained reality. Nothing can be outside of or separate from everything in truth. The duality of cause and effect is in itself an ultimate oxymo-ron. What appears as separate (effects) still must remain part of everything (cause). This understanding is another good example of non-dual thinking. It reveals a higher level of perception wherein what we thought was "two" is now recognized as "one." We collapse the dualistic illusion of separation and opposites and perceive the Oneness out of which we only imagined twoness.

A major challenge in truly receiving this understanding is our belief, through our senses, that the Universe is objectively real. We are hypnotized inside the limits we imagined. One of the greatest justifications for this belief in a "solid" Universe, aside from our sensory experience, is the seeming continuity of the Universe over time. Time, a construct of mind along with everything else, is a particularly resilient illusion. It represents our imagined ability to separate events into a chain of cause-and-effect relationships. The notion of time reflects our total commitment to dive into the deepest aspects of separation in their seemingly infinite expressions. We see the same principle reflected in the science of fractals, where patterns in nature seem to repeat themselves on multiple scales into seeming infinity. Our belief in the "great separation" is supported largely by our belief in time.

It is the illusion of time that convinces us that the Big Oops is unfolding over billions of years, while in fact, due to its ontological impossibility, the Universe was over the moment it was imagined. From this premise, we could claim that "all events in the Universe in all timeframes are occurring simultaneously." I explored this notion in greater depth in the book *Navigating the Collapse of Time*, where the idea of linear time was deconstructed, shifting it from a horizontal model of past, present, and future stretched out over immense distances to a vertical model of time in alignment with the concept that all events have/are/will happen in a stretched out experience of now. This is not too hard to accept when we consider that all events, past, present, or future, are only ever experienced as "now" events. The past is only ever a memory we have now, and the future is only ever us in the now imagining a future that never arrives outside of now. The reason this is such mind-bending stuff is that the mind, in its current focus on linguistic and time-bound interpretations of its experience, has a difficult time letting go of its rational security blanket. "Where would I be without my time-bound concepts of self?" it shrieks in abject terror. "Relax," Spirit replies, "Where you'll find yourself once you give up these illusions is right where you started and in truth never left: at One with your Source; at peace with your Self and all Creation." As with most of life's lessons, if we truly look our fears square in the eyes we will find that they represent a mistake in our own minds—a mis-attribution of power over us, which in fact is quite groundless.

The ego, in its primary identification as a temporary physical body, trembles in fear at the notion of us somehow "dissolving" back into an amorphous, vague field of just being. "Sounds great, but what will happen to *me?*" Again, Spirit assures us, "Nothing real can or will be taken from you. If you desire the experience of individuation, you will have that experience. You may even have an experience of both individuation and complete immersion in the Oneness of All That Is, and be able to negotiate your existence on these and many levels simultaneously. So please don't be afraid. There is *no* fear in love, and love is who you are!"

Our perception of space is equally convincing within the dream. By separating the nuances of our experience here within time and space, we have created a master virtual playground, not unlike *The Matrix* movie series or a sophisticated virtual reality game. The key here is that this *will* be our experience until we desire something else—until we get sick and tired of losing the game and suffering, or until the Divine Will awakens and points our way home.

The seeming resilience of our fantasy-dream Universe should impress on you the real power we have to co-create realities, albeit largely unconsciously so far. If we can do all this with one ill-considered whim, what could we do when we really get our stuff together? Because of who we really are, our dip into fantasy seems to us to have taken 16.5 billion years to play out . . . so far. The good news is that the Divine Child is beginning to stir out of its dream state, and all signs indicate it is due to fully wake up.

FOUR

The Beginning of Wisdom

Is when I begin to see that I don't *really* understand anything here at all. I am beginning to
appreciate that my life, my world, and even myself are just
a set of perceptions that I adopted from others, my culture,
and my very limited thought-based interpretation of reality. I am beginning to doubt my own mind, at least how it
has been operating so far. It feels like the eggshell I have
been comfortably dozing in is beginning to crack because
I am outgrowing it! And I don't know yet what I am to
become.

This is an exciting yet potentially frightening place
to come to. Undoubtedly, we approach this point of
honest self-assessment many times, but quickly retreat
into the safety of the "known." This works temporarily to
dispel the anxiety that seems to bubble up along with self-
honesty, yet part of me knows I'm only fooling myself and
putting off the inevitable.

The Light has risen over the horizon and there's no going back now. It is beginning to peek through the cracks in the curtain, and my first glimpse of the Light through sleeping eyes tells me awakening is unpreventable now. Yes, I can turn over in my slumber and pretend the Light isn't there. But it's just too late to go fully back to sleep, so I ultimately throw off the covers and face a new day. In today's world, the alarm clock of global change, political and economic chaos, and seemingly unsolvable social problems, all instantly reported online, is making it practically impossible to ignore that we are overdue for collective awakening, like it or not.

When I accepted that all the understanding and knowledge I had gained in this life really added up to zilch, I allowed space for something new and different to emerge. As long as our awareness is "full" of thought constructs and ego distractions, there's no room for anything else. We have said the ego is an illusion, and this remains true. But it is a very tenacious and even vicious illusion in its omni-directional survival programming.

The ego will become particularly active when it senses you are about to expose, understand, and abandon it. It will throw up all kinds of resistance to you changing, in whatever form best suits its purpose. These may include "special" relationships that are threatened by your awakening, old memories of past "sins" and the guilt they seem to carry, or "rational excuses" for why you must stay the same (for your own safety, security, or sanity, or for the sake of someone else). What all these and other ego-ploys have in common is that they all carry an element of fear . . . a sense of "If you follow your heart and do this, what will happen then?" as if the ego knows your future and in its benevolence is trying to protect *you* from certain doom.

If you find yourself at this impasse of either staying with the familiar or leaping off the cliff into the great unknown, let me encourage you that you cannot fail, even if you "fail" in the ego's judgment. Spirit (the Divine, God, your Higher Self . . .) will *always* respond to your sincere desire to awaken. In effect, this Spirit *is You in your awakened state*. You will only ever experience your Self. We just didn't know who this capital "S" Self was for most of our human lives. We were satisfied with a temporary substitute "small S" self, at least until it failed to allow the Inner Spark to grow, as it must and will.

Shortly after I made this confession to myself (that I did not know or understand *anything*), I discovered, or was led to discover, the book *The Disappearance of the Universe* by Gary Renard.[5] Maybe the title grabbed me because *my* universe was disappearing! The ideas in the book literally pulled me into deeper parts of myself that I was not even aware of. At times, the ideas in Gary's book challenged my assumptions so much that I had to put the book down for a week or two and let the possibilities steep. I accepted,

....
5. Gary Renard, *The Disappearance of the Universe* (Carlsbad, CA: Hay House, 2002).

though, that if my fundamental beliefs about reality could be shaken by these new ideas, maybe my beliefs weren't so solid after all! So I would dive back into the work and eventually became a grateful student of the Course, which is what *Disappearance* is all about. Before we move forward, I want to note that even many long-term students of the Course report that they never really "got" the Course until they read Gary's book. It's highly recommended!

I had seen the Course before, but the religious language was a turnoff. I had "done my time" in dualistic religion, and was over it a long time ago. But Gary's book was written in such a friendly and conversational way that I was able to absorb what was being offered and put aside my own biases and prejudices, including my resistance to becoming or even being regarded by others as "religious" in any sense of the word.

The Course acknowledges that it is not for everyone, but everyone eventually takes it. It does not suggest that there will be a Course book in every motel room from now to eternity, but does imply that the *ideas* in the Course have universal application, and will appear to those who are ready in whatever form their minds can accept at the time. The Course says that "We all go home" eventually. In truth, we have already made it home, outside the illusion of time. There are over seven billion paths on the planet now, and they *all lead home*. Some paths just appear to take longer. Our Creator is infinitely patient in His undying love and confidence in His Creation. Can we thus truly judge the path that anyone is on?

So as we become honest with ourselves, we may find great resistance in admitting the three hardest words in the English language: "I was mistaken . . ."

Once the choice to awaken has been formed, it's all uphill from here on, despite a few road bumps. Support for our decision to wake up continues to flow toward us, and we receive as much as we are willing to take in at any given time. Just as we see certain forms repeated in Nature, like the "Golden Mean" ratio and Plato's five geometric solids, so it appears our progress toward home spirals and accelerates upward through cycles of experience. It may even appear that we are revisiting "old issues," yet from a slightly higher elevation. As we ascend we find particular learning aids assist us on our journey. The great non-dual works of the past, the Tao and Vedanta for example, have helped many on the path of ascension. For me, the Course can be counted among these great gifts to humanity.

The Course offered me a continual flow of insights, all "adjusted" to fit my needs in the moment, and it continues to do so today and every day. I began to see that all of my perceptions were based on nothing but past conditioning. I bring my past to every present moment experience as soon as I apply a concept to the experience or label what seems to be going on. Although my reliance on thinking has been deceptively functional, I am now starting to appreciate how small my thought-conditioned world truly is. How many insights and opportunities do I miss simply because my view is obscured by an old, outdated roadmap? William Blake said, "If the doors of perception were cleansed we would see everything as it is, infinite." Thus, if the doors of perception are shut, we see everything as it isn't: limited and separate.

Earlier in this book I discussed psychologists' studies on perception and their attempts to reduce our perceptual world to an effect of internal biochemical events. This notion is limiting enough, sentencing each of us, as it were, to our own private universes or in some cases hells. Reliance on thought alone is limiting because our only resource for perceiving meaning is a past based itself on limited perception. This touches on a very deep concept addressed in the Course and other non-dual thought systems: that time is a particularly tricky illusion. In our desire for and belief in our experience of separation, we created time in order to separate our experiences from each other, the better to savor them, I suppose. As Einstein is credited with saying, "The only reason for time is so that everything doesn't happen at once." But what if it does, and we are simply "wasting time" indulging our illusions while paying the price with our suffering?

By saying time is an illusion, do I mean that time does not exist? Outside of our imaginations and projections, the answer is a ringing *yes*. All of your experiences, no matter whether you call them past, present, or future, only ever happen in an experience of *this moment*. The true value of this moment is that it is the only time wherein you can choose to awaken. The past is only ever a present memory and the future a present possibility. If time is my only "reality filter" and I drag this belief unchallenged into every present moment experience, then I don't see anything as it truly is. I am walking forward facing backward. No wonder I stumble!

Applied to myself, then, these ideas indicate that I don't really know myself as I truly am. I have gathered a number of *ideas* about who I am, many of which were supplied by my own ego or handed to me by well-meaning others living out of their "book of time." I have projected my entire life's movie from within my own mind even while my mind struggled to make meaning out of its dazed state of supposed separation. Although this realization is a shock and challenge to all I have assumed to be "real" up to this point, another part of me is trembling in joyful anticipation of the freedom I sense from all the suffering this time prison has created. Part of me is dissolving and another part of me, peeking out from the cracks in my assumptions, remembers and knows that "all is in Divine order."

It has been said that the end of a thing is better than the beginning. The mind really does feel much more in control with this kind of "either-or" thinking. Yet I am learning that the dualistic musings of my mind often mask a broader view that substitutes "and" for "either-or." In other words, newer levels of perception can often be gained by joining former contradictory ideas, and in imagining a context where both seeming opposites could be true. Perhaps my sense of loss of meaning, the end of my former confidence in my own self-image that came with realization that I didn't really understand anything at all, can be viewed as the starting point for an entirely new adventure into a fresh answer to the perennial question, "Who am I?" Words that come close to describing my excitement include *freedom, peace, purpose,* and *wholeness.* I have decided the promise of newness, yet unknown, is worth the risk of shedding what no longer "fits" anyway. The past is appearing to me like a moldy old book, whereas the future is arriving in each moment with indescribable light and limitless joy.

FIVE

Back to the Cause

I am now seeing that the world and people "out there" are merely projections of the state of my own mind. The suffering and conflict I see in the world is mirroring back to me the suffering and conflict I have taken on in my dream state of separation. In realizing that my own mind is the source and cause of *all* my experiences, I am empowered by the notion that I need not go anywhere outside myself to correct my errors. I have found the reins to my own wild horse mind. My willingness to face and accept an uncomfortable truth has placed me in a place where I can consciously direct my experience of the world by simply making new choices moment by moment. There's a new purpose to this dream.

Come to think of it, all the places I have been and teachers I have met or read have all led me back to myself. Each learning event expanded this sense of unlimited self as much as I would allow. Any vision or revelation that seemed to come from an outside source was simply released from the place it waited within, imprisoned in my own sleeping mind.

If my projection literally makes my perception (as the Course states often), I must return my attention to the creative part of my mind as both the source of suffering and the place of liberation. If I am showing a movie and there is a glaring flaw in the image on screen, do I set about trying to erase the flaw in the image, or look to the projector for the cause of the problem? And who in their right mind would tolerate such a flaw any longer once its source was clearly identified?

Perhaps there is value in stepping back at this point and asking, "What happened to the mind that it would project such an insane dream as this world of suffering?" Again, we return to our metaphysical premise that the Universe as we see it is the result of our choice to experience something "other than" absolute Wholeness. In thinking that we actually pulled it off, we accepted ourselves in a less-than-whole state of being. It is the belief in our separateness that literally "split" our minds into the deluded part that bought in to the whole fantasy of separation, and the part that remained sane in the Presence of Itself as One with the Source. That's why I said earlier, "We are all schizophrenics here." That is simply the nature of being in the world we made in order to live out this particular dream. Remember, though, that this illusion is not judged as "bad" by Source, and we are in no way seen as bad for falling asleep. Think again of the image of a caring parent gazing with absolute love at their sleeping child. Yes, the child may be having crazy dreams, or even nightmares, but the parent knows nothing is happening in truth, and that the child will soon awaken, refreshed and back to themselves as a happy and perfect "chip off the old block." The parent in this case could be seen as Source or as your own perfect Self at One with Source, which remains fully conscious even as you dream. In the metaphysics of Oneness, terminology gets somewhat vague as all concepts begin to merge. This is why silence is so valued in practically all spiritual traditions and practices—we leave thought behind we make room for what can only be experienced.

The great hope and empowering aspect of this new perspective on my mind is that if the world at large is equally the result of my and everybody else's projections (as masterfully illustrated in the movie *Inception*, by the way), then there is great hope that by my efforts and example, I may start a chain reaction of awakening that will benefit everyone. After all, we are all still One, we all still want the same thing, and we are driven by the same Divine Will. Why shouldn't the actions of one affect all? Once we truly get this, it may occur to us that there is very little value in doing anything in this world that is not in alignment with Oneness. The word "healing" means "returning to wholeness." Those who have experienced their own healing, no matter on what level, soon realize that they want to pursue this healing from now on. This is likely why many spiritual types also populate the healing arts. As the outcome of our healing path is already assured, all we really can do of any consequence in this dream once we choose to awaken is save time and reduce suffering along the way.

As John Lennon offered in his song "Imagine," the Creation of a New World of peace and harmony begins in our imagination. Begin to "see" your life and relationships as free from negative projections and expectations. Begin to liberate your friends, family, community, nation, and world from your fearful projections. Don't buy in to others' fearful projections either. Know that the temporary insanity of this world is simply a stage we are passing through on our way to becoming fully what we already are, but have lost sight of. Forgive those who know not what they do, or why they do it. The call for love of even the "worst" behaviors cannot go unheeded. As One we are created, remain, and must remember. Paradoxically, our true freedom is realized when we understand that there is no freedom of choice when it comes to the changeless reality You are.

What kind of world does an awakened mind create for itself? One in which there is no conflict (all conflict is between illusions only), no greed (fear of lack within a limitless Universe), no disease (the ego's war on the body), no inequality (if you are another me and there is no real separation between us, why would I hurt, neglect, or deny myself?), and no war (the acting out of a fearful ego against imagined "enemies"). Our elders of today live in a world of technology they could not even imagine a decade ago.

Why not create a world of peace that we may have a hard time imagining today, yet *must happen* if we are to survive and mature into the fullness of our birthright as Divine Beings?

METAPHYSICAL MOMENT . . .

As you entertain these ideas, allow the feeling they may elicit within you to come fully into your awareness. Recognize this feeling as a "homecoming" that happens on the inner planes. Know that the more you allow this inner feeling of wholeness and safety to be your conscious experience, the more your mind will naturally lean toward these understandings, and begin to create and attract opportunities for you to live their truths—in your body, your relationships, and your world.

Not that "a better life" or "a better world" is the goal in awakening from all illusions. This focus alone is stopping short of the goal, and can actually present an ego trap that delays your full awakening. Would you rather "fix" an old dream, or wake up to reality? A better life and world, what the Course calls "the happy dream," will result naturally from our return to the true power of choice allowing us to recover the fullness of our original nature: peace, love, harmony, and limitless creative potential.

Remember that the mind was whole at one time, and in truth, it still is. It decided within its absolute freedom to question this wholeness, and is getting a good taste of the effects of that decision. Nothing the mind experiences in this dream-life has affected its ability to choose from a state of absolute freedom. Why put off choosing reality any longer? Unless of course there's a form of suffering that still looks worthwhile. Not even Creator would deny you your freedom to experience whatever you choose. That's how much you are loved. Of course Creator knows nothing is really going on here at all! One day we will all laugh about this together. In the meantime, one of the best gifts we can give ourselves as we choose the path of awakening is the determination to take full responsibility (the ability to respond from truth) for ourselves by seeing *everything* as originating from the level of Mind, and committing on focus our time and attention to its recovery. Your mind is the ultimate level of cause—all else is merely effect.

SIX

Cultivating Silence and the Rediscovery of the Will

Having come this far in our discussion, I am going to assume that your inner will to awaken is activated. If it isn't, I doubt if you'd still be reading! Before discussing the value of spiritual practice and cultivating silence, I want to reinforce this activation of Will as a key prerequisite to all that follows.

If the mind is the horse, the Will is the rider. Most of us live with a wild horse in our stable and thus we are not very stable at all. The mind that is not under the control of the Will is under its own control, and thus is out of control. The "thinking" mind, in its inherent blindness to reality, can never break free of limitations on its own strength alone. Another part of us must come on board to help us over the hump of our own hypnosis. This is the Will, or what some may call desire.

We all share common desires: happiness, health, freedom, etc. These are really desired outcomes of what we truly desire beneath these specifics. We really desire union. We want to know and remember that we are *not* disconnected from our Source or each other. Thus we are not truly guilty of our "crazy idea" to experience separation. It is *all okay!* The Divine got over it a long time ago—as soon as the separation appeared to happen, actually. In our deeply held but unfounded guilt, though, we believe that we must suffer for our mistake. This mistaken idea is at the root of all notion of sacrifice, an unfortunate aspect of many spiritual traditions. And so we do suffer until we remember otherwise.

The recovery of the Will is also the reinstatement of love as our guiding light. It starts with loving ourselves enough to see that we, and nobody else, are hurting ourselves. By stubbornly holding on to ideas about ourselves that are simply not true, we blindly perpetuate the suffering that seems to come to us from outside. Our minds are the "attractor factor" for whatever we magnetize into our movie script. Once the courage to see and accept this appears and we see the light of our own self-sabotaging system as based on mistaken thinking, we can make a new choice. Recognizing how many times we are offered to see this "new choice potential" over and over again speaks to me quite clearly of the eternal patience of the Divine. Your Creator's confidence in you is so unshakable that *nothing you have done or could ever do* changes Its/His/Her mind about you.

It is the Will within, that spark of remembrance we all carry, without exception, that provides the courage for us to accept total responsibility for our every experience. For until we do, there is no alternative but to project our pain outward and remain victim to "the world outside."

The good news about this Will is that you already have it. It is part of your Divine birthright. It isn't actually "your" Will in a personal sense, although you do need to agree to activate it. In truth, "your" Will is the same as "my" Will and is One with our Creator's Will. Just one Will between us all, driving all life on this planet! "How is that?" you may rightfully ask. "How can war, poverty, and illness be God's Will?"

First of all, our perception of the division of "good and evil" is the result of our descent into duality consciousness, or the belief in opposites and polarities. Remember the tree of knowledge in Genesis? Yep—that's what the analogy is talking about. We took on "duality consciousness" at a certain point. Before that, all we perceived was perfection. Nothing out of place, no harm possible . . . heaven! Whether this cultural story is literal or allegory doesn't really matter. It does capture the essence of our apparent conundrum of being caught in the middle of the choice between the polarities of darkness and light as polarized opposites.

The Course offers a fresh perspective on duality by portraying it as impossible and thus illusory. It was only a perception or misperception of the mind that wanted to experience separation. There's that Will again! How better to play out our fantasy than to separate every experience into an endless varying continuum between two opposite poles? The perception that our chosen illusion is so convincingly comprehensive and complex despite paradoxes and contradictions only attests to the power of the mind that is dreaming it, even when misdirected by a false desire for something impossible.

From the Course's non-dual perspective, *all behavior arises from love*. Quite simply, good behavior is an expression of love and bad behavior is a call for love, or the result of the lack of love in a given experience. We only act "badly" when a part of us knows it doesn't have to be this way—that there is always a loving alternative, but we are not experiencing it *now*. Consider that if we knew not of love in the first place, we would not suffer in its absence. But we do, and we act out in an attempt to recover that love. All this realization takes is a little patience, a little compassion for ourselves, and a willingness (which is Divine!) to see things differently. Can you do that? Of course you can! You were made in love, by love, to return to love. This is the beginning and end of everyone's story.

Some may feel their personal Will is too weak to sustain a whole new perspective on life, especially as broad and sweeping a view as the one presented in the Course. Some days we stand strong; other days we seem to drift backward. I encourage you to consider that our Will is not limited by any feelings we may have about it. The Divine only needs to see 1 percent willingness in order to activate and start the process of our awakening and ultimate return to the state of wholeness. I am beginning to think that even 1 percent willingness *to be willing* would suffice! You could say our Will is a holographic piece of the Divine Will, and in this sense the whole power of Divine Will is in every tiny fragment, no matter how small it may appear.

I like to call this turning point the place where we shift from disempowerment and the tyranny of the ego to the power of the Will within—"flipping in" as opposed to "flipping out" at the world and others. When we realize that life's patterns are coming *from* us, not *to* us, we find ourselves at a fork in the road. One direction leads back to the way we came with more of the same bumps and potholes; another leads to unimagined adventures and discovery. One way guarantees more suffering; the other promises to lead away from all suffering. The choice of which road to take may not be easy, but it really is as simple as the choice between love and fear. And no one but *you* can make this choice. If anyone could make it for you, you would not be in your power. You would not be as you are created.

The knowledge that "my world is as I am" leads to a dawning suspicion that my thoughts of blame, attack, defense, revenge, and fear are not only unreal—they are not even necessary. I become aware that my "automatic" judgments are actually unconscious decisions that I made and can just as easily let go of. There is a growing sense of inner strength as I commit to myself with newfound courage borne of a will recovered from the smothering layers of conditioning. Who cares if I no longer appear to fit into my former world? Who wants to be aligned with insanity? Although I can no longer agree with or be around those who choose to linger in their self-made hells (at least for a little while), I can release them from my judgment of what is "right" for them because I know that at the appointed time, they too will be given every opportunity to see the light ahead and choose that fork in the road marked "love." After all, the One Will that has awoken in me dwells just as powerfully within them. It is a seed whose time of fruition is appointed and must inevitably come.

Ironically, the ending of the drama comes after I take full responsibility for all the dramas in my life. This does not imply that we must dive headfirst into the "doodoo" out of a sense of sacrifice or self-punishment, but we can step back from our chosen role as victim and see if there is not a bigger picture . . . and there *always is*. When I can truly say and mean "All I ever experience is myself," I have opened a fundamental portal to my own liberation and recovery of sanity. I am a victim to nothing other than my own thoughts, and my thoughts are subject to my Will, which is Divine. And if this is true for me, it must also be true for everyone—all those I have called "other" than me are only experiencing themselves, and thus can be held blameless for anything they may have thought or done outside of the truth, which has simply not been born into their conscious awareness (yet).

This knowledge releases me of the need to project any guilt hidden in my mind onto others and the world. Doing so will only hurt me and have no real effect on others, other than to further separate us. They can only experience themselves, as can I. Holding on to my pain cannot interfere with anyone's awakening but my own.

To extend this truth further, if I only ever experience myself, but I still experience pain and suffering, does this mean I *am* pain and suffering? Or does it mean I am not yet "my Self" in its ultimate and pure expression? Is this why I still appear to be in time— in order to give myself time to awaken gently and bring others with me? This too, I must experience, but there's some interference, some aspects of a "false self" that clearly need to be addressed in order for me to continue growing. Is this why I still appear to be here in the dream, even though I know it cannot be real?

Even as I begin to grasp the bigger picture and embrace the truth about myself; even as I have wonderful experiences that reflect back to me my growing sense of wholeness, I still have "stuff" to deal with. How do I reconcile this paradox? How can I be in the world while I am clearly not *of* the world?

This is where having some kind of spiritual practice comes in. If we are still experiencing time, then why not put time to work *for* us? I find that having a time each day to "go within" is crucial to my continued remembering of these ideas throughout the day. Otherwise, the "stuff of life" can simply be too overwhelming, easily pulling us down into the eddies and vortices of day-to-day challenges. You will find most practices that involve the silencing of the mind to be most effective. As we release the attachment to thought, thought becomes less "sticky" and we find it easier to become the neutral observer of our own thoughts and judgments as they arise rather than being led around by the nose by them. Think of Spirit (Love, your Higher Self) in the image of a dove. It will only land in a peaceful place. As long as the nest of your mind is restless, it will simply hover above you, out of view and out of mind. Welcome it home.

SEVEN

Practicalities

We now enter a discussion of the "practicalities" of awakening from the dream of separation. The ideas discussed so far are critical to allowing the space for the Will to activate and awaken. Once started, the process must complete. However, as we still seem to be experiencing time, space, and our bodies, there must be some practical means to staying actively involved and connected with the awakening process. This is where having some kind of practice to support our decision becomes crucial to our effectively saving time and reducing suffering.

As the term "practice" implies, we have not yet stepped fully into mastery. Like virtuoso musicians, we may have inherent gifts, but we still need to develop the skills to fully manifest those natural talents. Even a reincarnated Mozart would still need piano lessons at some stage. We need to practice regularly to get to mastery. The value of a spiritual practice is in the repetition. We are using the fact that the mind can be conditioned by repetition to our benefit.

We have many choices of spiritual practice. Even mainstream religions have their "mystical" traditions and can offer practices that work. You will have to look outside the public face of these religions to find them, and they are often buried in the history books or fringe elements of these religions. Christianity has its contemplative traditions, Judaism the Kabala, Islam the Sufi traditions, and so on.

One crucial element of any effective spiritual practice is that it must bring the mind to moments of silence. Buddhist mindfulness practice is an excellent example. We need to be able to glimpse the light between the prison bars of our own thinking. It is only in silence that we "hear" that part of the mind that is not invested in separation, that still rests in the fields of unconditioned creativity and potential. Words, thoughts, and ideas are the projected images of the separated ego onto the screen of our mind. We can use words or thoughts to bring us to the door of silence, but once in, we must leave them behind. We no longer need a key once the door is open. It gets tricky, however, when we finally enter silence, immediately and we think, "This must be silence!" D'oh!

On the way to silence, we may see images, colors, or hear sounds. These are products of the experience-generating mind. When we simply notice these things without the compulsion to give them meaning, we are becoming the silent witness of our experiences. The part that notices these things without personal identification is not attached to these things. The "right" part of our mind is saying to the "wrong" (mistaken or unawakened) part, "This is not my highest choice. I do not exist to suffer. I exist to become all That I Am, so I choose peace instead of this . . ."

THE BREATH: THE DOORWAY TO "NOW"

As many traditions illustrate, the breath is a tremendous ally in cultivating silence. We have noted that thinking is time-bound. Thus our thoughts are constantly pulling us away from this clear and open present moment, either through guiltily ruminating over the past or fearfully anticipating the future. The ego has corralled thought almost exclusively into its camp for the purpose of keeping a limited time-bound self-image at the forefront of our awareness.

The ego is not evil; it is simply a temporary blockage to our fullness of being. In its temporary nature, the ego is essentially a "functional illusion." On the upside, you could say the ego keeps us from waking up prematurely, as we all have a perfect time appointed for our awakening. Just as the butterfly abandons the old cocoon, the awakened Soul has no use for an ego at all.

By nature, thinking must engender some degree of fear, however subtle or unconscious. This is because thoughts create separation in our imagination of time and space. Any notion, nuance, or remembrance of separation resonates on a deep level with our terror-filled memory of the "big separation" event that we believe happened in our shared dream-illusion of the Creation of the Universe.

This is why concepts alone, even those in so-called "holy" books or scriptures, have contributed to so much division and suffering in the world. Literalism or scripture worship is a serious impediment to true spiritual growth. We mistake the map for the territory and end up settling for the map alone. We even create conflicts and wars over over whose 'map' is superior. Concepts themselves can only divide—as we have noted, they are essentially divisive by nature. There will always be an opposite idea or opinion that must be considered as equally possible or as an antithesis by the dualistic mind. However, the Spirit or essence toward which "right-minded" concepts point can only unite where they are welcomed. The ego loves when we isolate and idolize an idea or a set of rules or beliefs as being complete and whole in itself, as it knows we can waste eons in that mental cul-de-sac that ultimately goes nowhere.

A very simple and effective tool for bringing our attention into the present moment (which is the only time we truly experience our place of decision and thus power) and away from time-bound thinking is the natural breath. Surprise! The path to wholeness was literally right under our noses all along!

Biofeedback research first conducted in the 1970s discovered that the breath and the mind are cybernetically connected: The state of mind is reflected in the breath patterns, and consciously changing our breathing changes our state of mind. This is the basis of classic biofeedback and many stress reduction practices. The Vedic practice of Pranayama, an ancient form of yoga, has taken the breath-consciousness link and refined it into an exact science and powerful spiritual practice.

If you are interested in jumping into a practice right away without doing further research, I would like to offer a simple non-religious practice that "works" just as well as many more complex systems.

BREATH MEDITATION FOR STRESS RELIEF

The purpose of this simple meditation is to help establish the experience of inner peace by quieting the mind.

When we experience ourselves as the source of inner peace, we become less anxious and feel more at home with ourselves. Happiness, we discover, is not something we need to pursue or gain, but is our natural state. This realization can help the "seeker" in us relax by recognizing that what we seek is already within us. By practicing this simple breath meditation once or twice daily, your inner peace will begin to flow outward, spontaneously affecting the world around you without any other special effort on your part. Simply follow these suggestions. The breath meditation is a simple, foundational technique to which you can add other techniques as you progress on your inner path. The time you take to do this is your gift to yourself . . . the value is only in *doing* it. Find a quiet, comfortable place where you can sit undisturbed for fifteen or twenty minutes. You may want a watch or clock nearby so you check the time.

1. Sitting comfortably with your eyes closed, begin to simply notice your easy, natural breath. There is no special effort here—just watch your breathing and begin to mentally label each breath cycle from one to ten.

2. When you notice your attention has wandered to a thought (which it will—you will quickly discover that the thinking part of the mind has a mind of its own!), simply notice and label this experience as "thinking" and go back to the previous step. Do not judge yourself for "not doing it right." That's just more thinking. Observe, be present, and simply choose the breath over thinking as often as you need to.

3. As simple as this seems, you are doing two profound things. First, you are experiencing yourself not as the thinker or the thought, but as the Silent Observer, who is choosing repeatedly to bring attention back to the breath and now. This is you, the "choice maker," and Divine Will in action. Second, whatever you can observe, you are not that thing . . . you've created a gap between the observer and the observed; in this case the thinking process. This gap is an opening in your attention and will lead to your liberation from mental torture and psychological suffering, which is

at the root of most human suffering. Thoughts, we discover, are based either in memory, which is the past, or planning, which is the future. The past and future are mind-created, and don't really exist outside of your thinking. As you continue your practice, you will begin to experience little patches of pure silence, which will expand in frequency and intensity. This is where we experience ourselves as pure and peaceful awareness. This peace tends to carry over spontaneously into our daily lives.

That's all! Remember to keep a kind and easy attitude toward yourself. The breath meditation is not a challenge to master; it is simply a way to learn to experience the deep well of inner peace waiting within each of us. Listen to what the silence has to offer you. Experiencing true silence will leave you feeling that everything is okay and there is nothing real to fear.

Each time you go into the silence, you bring a little bit more back into the drama of the dream world. Ultimately, you will be in the silence even when you appear to be busy and interacting with the world outside of you. It is when we are inwardly silent that we can allow all things to be what they are without any burden of judgment or reaction necessary. We flow through situations, keenly aware of opportunities to bring peace into our experiences.

The analogy of allowing the stream to carry you where it will rather than trying to swim against it is apt here. You develop trust as you surrender each moment to the river of Spirit moving through you. Plans become more open-ended, so that you are not thrown off balance as circumstances change (as they always will in the dream). What can change so readily cannot be essentially real. The changeless in you is your Divine Self. Make knowing this your goal and you will be pursuing the greatest goal anyone here can possibly aspire to . . . your own awakening.

LEARNING TO BE IN THE NOW

You can extend the ideas of this simple practice into everyday life. Whenever you experience an inner conflict or discomfort, choose instead of diving in and wrestling one idea against another to turn your attention inward and take three slow, deep breaths. Even this simple, healthy moment of detachment will create a little gap in the flow of your thinking to enable light to break through to your willing awareness. You could say you are making room for your intuition or "whole mind" to enter the party, rather than just letting the wild dogs of your conditioning to determine the experience.

Another cognitive tool is to think of time as operating vertically rather than horizontally. I covered this idea more completely in my first book and touched on it somewhat in this book already, but briefly, here's the idea. We were all taught at one time or another to think of time as organized on a horizontal axis. Textbook "timelines" were depicted as horizontal, right? This model seems to create the impression that the past and future make up most of what we call time, while the present moment is just this seemingly puny and inconsequential blip on the vast continuum of time.

How disempowering is this? What choices can we make in this little "dot" of now that could in any way change or alter the "facts" of past and future? The ego loves this model, because it gives practically all our power to the ego, the grand master of time, using our past to keep us guilty and our future to keep us fearful.

I suggest you take this horizontal model in your mind and begin to turn it slowly around until it becomes vertical. You now have a model that more closely represents the non-dual idea that time is an illusion and everything is happening at once, all in a stretched out experience of "now." If time has any meaning at all (and recall that *we* give all the meaning anything has for us ourselves), it is that time is only actually experienced as "now" . . . ever. Not only does the vertical model of time re-establish you in your place of power (the Course states that "Now is the closest approximation to eternity we have in time"), but it brings all past and future memories and thoughts into this moment, where they can be examined, tossed out as worthless, or reinterpreted to be more supportive of truth. "The past is not what it used to be," a wise person once said to me (so I ended up marrying her!).

The ramifications of living vertically are vast and profound. Take illness: Mind-body researchers tell us that illness is the result of messages we send to the body. The body does not *cause* disease. The body is a neutral communication system that takes all its orders from you! When we are able to discern the origin of an illness in an unpleasant memory (emotional trauma, for example) and see this memory as simply something from the past held in the now, it is easier for us to examine and rethink the decision made in the "past-now" and thereby change the message the body thinks it has to manifest. In our healing practice, called "Mind Field Repatterning," we often find sources of present problems held in deep, unconscious memories of childhood or so-called past lives. I say "so-called" as, according to the vertical model, *all* lifetimes are being lived simultaneously—past and future lives included—so they aren't really that far away . . . just held somewhere in our vast, present moment memory.

Thinking of all time happening at once simultaneously collapses the belief in separation of space as well—time and space, according to Einstein, are inextricably linked. It becomes easier to grasp the notion that the entire Universe is a single projected image of a unified mind while being held in that mind at the same time, with no separation between the observed and the observer. Recently, scientists have discovered the physical Universe is split right down the middle by a dividing line—all galaxies on one side spin to the left, and all galaxies on the other spin to the right. What better reflection of our brains, split both on the physical level between two hemispheres and split in consciousness between the experience of separation and the knowledge of truth?

The vertical model of time is also consistent with our metaphysical precept that the Big Bang occurred all at once, and was over the moment it was imagined (because of its inherent impossibility). *But . . .* because we wanted the experience, and because of Who we are and the creative power our decisions carry, this "momentary lapse of reason" appears to have taken billions of years to unfold. Hence time is a great preserver of the illusion of separation, and time is just an idea to be re-examined and challenged in light of what we are discovering.

This section on learning to live in the now is a great example of how words and concepts alone ultimately fail to deliver the goods. You may agree intellectually with the idea of mental silence and its value, but without actually *doing it* these are really just empty thoughts. In order to undo time, we need to use our experience of time toward that purpose; thus we choose to use time to get rid of time altogether. We can do this by devoting time to silence and our lives to forgiveness. We'll have more to say about that later.

If you do not yet have a spiritual practice to try out, or are undecided about the best practice for you, do the breath meditation described above (pages 81–84). Even if time constraints do not allow for regular inner work, do it anyway. If you choose to support yourself in new ways and others can't or won't understand, do it anyway. If your life really goes to hell, and everything you thought was meaningful starts to dissolve before you, do it anyway. To paraphrase the Course, "What is real cannot be destroyed, what is unreal (and thus subject to constant change) does not exist. Really getting this is finding the peace of God." If you are not getting this, why not ask for help? You are really only asking for what is yours already, so there's no extra effort on God's part to answer you. He/She/It is much more willing to give than we are to receive. Yet receiving is how we give to ourselves, and, hey . . . you are worth it!

EIGHT

Going Deeper: Recognizing Illusion

Let's face it, we love our illusions! We are delighted and entertained by magic. The fantasies we crave provide welcome relief from the mundane humdrum same-old-same-old of everyday life. "Thank God it's Friday!" we cry as we rush from our cubicles to the excitement and unpredictability of yet another wild weekend. Or we retreat to the safety of our familiar relationships, hobbies, or sports to provide the novelty and diversion we need to stay sane. Many of us even prefer the stimulation of shallow or meaningless relationships over being alone with our uncomfortable thoughts and feelings. Being alone is considered antisocial and weird, and it is unpleasant for those who are simply addicted to distraction.

We even think of "disillusionment" as a negative, even though it clearly means the end of an illusion and the dawning of reality. I suppose I can understand why people who exist in the predominant pre-fab cookie cutter corporate culture—who think of this plastic paradise as reality—need to escape into exciting fantasies. Without a break from the loony-bin world, you might end up in . . . well, the loony bin!

A mirror is a good illustration of how the illusions of this world deceive us so well. A mirror always provides an accurate depiction of whatever is being reflected, except for one small detail: the image is backward! If you are right-handed in the "real" world, you will be left-handed in the mirror world.

Recall how we talked about how the outer world is in fact a projection of the mind. I am extending the idea to include the notion that what is being "played back" to us on the screen of the world is more accurately a mirror image of our inner world. Thus we are seeing reverse images and perceptual distortions everywhere we look. Does this explain why the world seems to have practically everything wrong? Accurate on first glance perhaps, but on closer inspection, it's all bass ackwards!

Nowhere is this more evident than in our dysfunctional public institutions. In true Orwellian fashion, we have "defense" departments that are chronically addicted to war, a "health care" system that operates (pun intended) largely as a "disease care" system that incidentally kills many more than it heals (search *iatrogenic disease*—or death by medicine), an "education system" that has become no more than a job readiness program for corporations, and a "food industry" that has so denatured and processed our food that modern societies are dying of starvation while overfed on junk. Something is fundamentally off in this mirror world.

Functioning in the modern world has become like walking through the hall of mirrors at a carnival. Everywhere you turn you find distorted images of what you and your life were intended to be. We are manipulated by lies ("advertising"), propaganda ("news"), and sick fantasies ("entertainment") to the point that, in the modern techno-societies at least, we have become more and more like the distorted images we are offered on a daily basis. All of this is being driven by "market forces" and the capitalist business model that has infected our culture to the point of consuming us like a cancer, destroying the very body that gave it life in the pursuit of limitless growth. Like cancer in the body, however, this cancer, though globally pervasive and seemingly unstoppable, has its origin in the collective mind. And it is on the level of the mind where we will choose something much better for ourselves and the generations to come. There is no reason to wait for the healing to begin. This change can start now on the level of your own mind.

Do not underestimate the power of one. Declare your independence from the mirror world and set the example to those still lost in the maze. From the perspective of Oneness, all minds are joined; each of us is a holographic micro-mind with all the capacities and potentials of the collective mind. Each of us has the ability and "connections" to affect the collective in ways that are hard to appreciate from the stance of our seeming separateness.

The collective mind, recognized by Jung, operates in the "fourth dimension" or mental plane. According to Barbara Hand Clow's model, the mind is not subject to the same limited Newtonian Laws of the 3D material realm, but instead operates according to established quantum laws and principles.[6] This is one reason why our collective illusions are the most pernicious and hardest to recognize *as* illusions. Deepak Chopra called the collective movie of the world as following the script according to "the hypnosis of social conditioning." The mirror world represents a conspiracy of micro-egos attempting to keep intact the collective agreement to stay asleep.

Social scientists are well aware of the dynamics of herd behavior and groupthink. They know that the unawakened human is driven by base instinct and the drive to survive. Market manipulators and advertising agencies have been playing on the base instincts of the puppet population for eons now. I wonder what new techniques they will employ when we all finally wake up and refuse to be led around by the nose as mindless "consumers." That is assuming there will be a corporate culture as we know it in the future at all.

Just like "really good" magicians, the best illusions are the most appealing and realistic. These deeply held illusions instill passionate allegiance from those caught in

....

6. Barbara Hand Clow, *The Alchemy of Nine Dimensions: The 2011/2012 Prophecies and Nine Dimensions of Consciousness* (Charlottesville, VA: Hampton Roads, 2004).

their web. Millions have been willing to die for the illusions propagated by war and the senseless separation of humanity into national, racial, or religiously profiled populations. How many have sacrificed themselves in defense of their right to be right? The last two thousand years of history are stained with the blood of those who took on the false identity and security offered by "in-group" identification with a nation, creed, or race as justification to take the lives of those who threaten their pet illusions. Must we put up with this institutionalized insanity any longer? Or are there indications that change is in the wind?

According to Western astrology, the last two-thousand-year period comprised the "Age of Pisces." The symbol of this passing age is two fish swimming in opposite directions in the same stream. What a perfect symbol for the era of separation, duality, and conflict of beliefs that has marked the last two millennia. The Age of Pisces has also been called the Age of Belief, during which countless numbers have been sacrificed to the gods of war over differing religious, economic, or political beliefs. Dying for an idea, much less killing for one? Sounds insane, I know. It is.

Beliefs, by the way, are simply a collection of unchallenged assumptions with a strong dose of identity mixed in. They are merely a substitute until replaced by knowledge, which is experiential. Beliefs provide mental scaffolding for those attempting to make a "self" out of thoughts. A belief is often conveniently pre-packaged and delivered with the bonus of group inclusion. Thus, many belief systems don't require much individual work or serious investigation in order to direct our lives—especially those beliefs one is simply "born into."

The psychoanalyst Eric Fromm's *Escape from Freedom* was all about this phenomenon.[7] Fromm described how, after the First and Second World Wars, large populations were suddenly thrown out of their familiar cultural contexts into unfamiliar spaces of freedom that were both foreign and uncomfortable. Many quickly gravitated to the pseudo-security of ready-made fanatical political or religious organizations rather than endure the uncertainty and responsibility that freedom created.

Beliefs are a substitute for knowledge. By "knowledge," I do not mean facts and data—that is mere information. Beliefs are sets of information based on the past that "work," until we *know*. Then we no longer need the support of a belief system. We have the experience, which offers unshakable confidence and clears the underlying fear and uncertainty of adopted beliefs. Beliefs in their weakness are vulnerable to perceived attack and thus require defense. Knowledge offers none, for to defend oneself admits weakness and uncertainty. To be defenseless in this sense is to demonstrate invulnerable strength, something that beliefs can only aspire to, but never achieve. The ego is an excellent example of an adopted belief system. It appears to

....

7. Erik Fromm, *Escape from Freedom* (New York: Holt and Company, 1941).

serve until we recognize and transcend its limits, and the ego is simply no longer seen as necessary.

Back to the astrological allegory. We are entering (or, depending on your source, have already entered) the Age of Aquarius wherein the water the Pisces fish were fighting in is now being poured out, freely and for all, by a female water bearer. I learned recently that although the image of Aquarius is that of the water bearer, Aquarius is in fact an air sign; the water being symbolic of the fifth alchemical element, Ether. Early scientists held the concept of Ether to explain the invisible energetic sub-matrix of matter, the "void" or vacuum from which matter emerges. In Mesoamerican culture, the terms *nagual* and *tonal* denote two parallel worlds that comprise the universe—the world of material objects and energy (the tonal) and the non-material or unmanifest world (the nagual). The shift to the astrological sign that symbolizes Ether mirrors the promise of a return to the awareness of the "unseen world"—the world of Spirit out of which Creation emerges. This is consistent with the notion of this era as being that of the "return of the Divine Feminine," or the awareness of the limitless loving potential that nurtures all manifestation.

David Wilcock, in his *Synchronicity Key,* has noted that on a grand galactic scale, specific vibrational tones in space generate geometries around the planet that in turn support different qualities of awareness for those here.[8]

....

8. David Wilcock, *The Synchronicity Key* (New York: Dutton, 2013).

The experimental science of Cymatics (Hans Jenny) has illustrated that sound generates geometries. Sound, in its purest sense, is simply repeating pressure waves that represent moving energy. Although audible sound, a small portion of the full spectrum of pressure wave energy, requires a medium such as air or water to be conveyed, there are "octaves" of sound energy that do not, and which pass easily through space. Just as visible light only makes up 1 percent of the entire electromagnetic range, so there is a lot more to sound than meets the ear.

Wilcock claims that a "new geometry" being generated around the planet is showing up in the form of a dodecahedron. The sound that is creating this form is galactic in origin. (I find it interesting that the Toltec term for the manifest realm is *the tonal*, just as a Biblical version of Creation began with *the Word*.) Wilcock says this particular geometric form supports the emergence of Ether as a new element representing Spiritual energy. It is both beautiful and encouraging to see so many ways of looking at the same thing. Even perceiving this, however, is subject to the Will. We only see what we want to see. And the choice remains simply between love or fear.

Each astrological age takes roughly two thousand years to complete. The shift into the Age of Aquarius is consistent with the idea of the ascension of Earth and the life she carries into the fifth dimension (of Divine perfection or Christ awareness) as an outcome of the Great Shift of the Ages. This is a natural cyclic event and part of a larger developmental process beyond Earth and humanity alone.

These ideas are also consistent with the anticipated Second Coming of Christ (by Christians at least). This event, predicted two thousand years ago, was not about the return of an avenging God-king with special interests, but rather about the birthing of unity in the One Mind we share and the "coming out" of the Light of our true nature on a planetary scale. This birthing includes *all of us* awakening to ourselves as Divine, perfect, innocent, and immortal. This event is only hard to imagine if we are still burdened by thinking we have no choice but to drag the past with us into the future. This is simply not true. We are free to choose.

I like to think of the Aquarian image as symbolizing free knowledge through direct experience that is being generously poured out to this planet *for all* in order to wash away the dualistic illusions of the past that have mired us in conflict and war. The fact that Aquarius is female adds to the allegory, as we witness the end of the "old boys network" in the form of the military-industrial complex and its indiscriminate thirst for blood and resources and a re-emergence of the Divine Feminine in a more caring, compassionate, and inclusive world.

As we begin to awaken to our true Spiritual nature, it is important that we commit to making room for truth by recognizing and releasing ourselves from our illusions. This is a systematic process. If all our illusions were torn away at once, we may not be of much use to anyone else here in Earth School, as happens, for example, in extreme drug-induced or ritual-driven premature "awakening."

Committing to the process of systematically dissolving our illusions gives time a whole new meaning and purpose. We are no longer doing time on prison planet Earth; we are *using* time to hasten the end of time's tyranny for all. This switches the whole image—time is no longer our enemy, but rather a friend who leads us toward opportunities to heal ourselves and each other one relationship at a time. Time, like the ego invested in it, is an illusion with a beginning, and so must surely have an end.

As noted, the three most convincing and thus challenging illusions we harbor are time (the belief that events are separated in time), space (the belief in the separation of objects by distance), and the body (the belief that I am limited to a temporary physical form.) It is our Divine destiny that we transcend these limitations. And we do not have to sit passively and wait for "eventually" to come. We can become proactive in our own awakening. In truth and as already noted, all we can realistically do here is save time and reduce the suffering. The outcome is already taken care of for us.

Coming to Earth School and experiencing time, space, and bodies is like reviewing an event that is already over. The race is over and everybody won. Now let's go to the movies and watch it all over again, post-game style, in order to better savor the experience and learn which strategies worked and which didn't.

You could say our number one job while we appear to be here in the dream of separation, time, space, and bodies is to clear away the debris of illusions and recover from the nightmare of separation. Life becomes quite simple when this is our purpose. It turns out that one of the richest resources for discovering and dispelling ("breaking the spell") of our illusions is again right under our noses in the form of our relationships; each relationship, whether fleeting or life-long, represents a perfect mirror of our current state of mind (should we choose to see it thus).

Think of your relationships as your projections. Then you can begin to take responsibility for your role in others' behavior, and recognize their actions either as an expression of or call for love from within yourself—nothing more than that. We'll discuss relationships later, as they offer a perfect doorway into the remembrance of the One Self and provide the most effective way to fast-forward the movie of our lives to the already-scripted "happy ending."

We can rely on our feelings (up or down?) to tell us when we are entertaining illusions. Even if initially pleasing, an illusion will always erode your sense of peace, as all illusions stem from the ONE BIG illusion that we are separate from our Creator and thus each other. Every illusion rests on this one illusion. All our "little" illusions echo the horror, guilt, and pain of the original illusion of separation. Thus illusions, though they may seem beneficial to the ego by affirming our "specialness," will always leave us sitting in ashes, as it were.

The ego part of your mind will try to convince you that your illusions are your friends, asking "Where and who will you be without them?" It was the uncertainty caused by our temporary insanity in the belief in our separation that gave rise to the ego in the first place. Without our asking "Who am I?" the ego would never have had a chance to reply. Fear of the unknown Self often keeps us from venturing beyond the little fences we have made around our small selves. Our fences are only temporary constructs that were planted in our minds as we struggled for meaning in our insane dreams of separation. "Don't hop the fence," cries the ego. It is time to ask why the ego is so afraid of what is outside. Why is it so insistent, sometimes violently so, that you not follow the urges of the inner Light to discover what is beyond the known?

The ego knows that everything it has to offer—feeling good, being special and powerful, having it all—is already yours in the form of Spirit's true gifts. These attributes and more are your unalterable inheritance. Don't settle for the ego's substitutes when what you truly want is already yours. As humans, we often don't know what is in our best interest. The mirror world has us convinced on many occasions that the "bad" events are just that—bad—until later on we realize that it if wasn't for that bad thing happening, we wouldn't have come to the wonderful place in which we find ourselves. Again, it's not that we *shouldn't* judge anything, it's that we *can't*.

Let me assure you that what lies out there in the great unknown is wonderful beyond imagination. Ask anyone who has come back from a near-death experience. The majority of these folks who came back to Earth School were highly reluctant to leave the place they discovered.

Their only comfort was that now they *knew* beyond all doubt that Heaven is real; it is their true home and destiny; and *this* place is not the real world at all!

When we get right down to basics, we learn that *all thought is illusion*, as thinking itself divides All That Is into little bite-sized pieces that substitute for the wholeness of reality. Being "okay" and accepting that "our thoughts are meaningless" is an incredibly liberating realization. This truth enables us to disengage from our inner dialogue and resign from the ego dramas that seem to drive many people crazy these days. Thought still happens, and you certainly need it to navigate 3D, but it becomes just a tool for your Awakened Self that is now in the driver's seat. Thought becomes simply another "functional illusion"—one you know will someday be totally unnecessary!

While on the subject of illusions, let's investigate another tragic yet common one. This is the belief in guilt, the idea that we must have royally screwed up in order to live a life of disconnection from our Source and each other. Somehow I must "deserve" the crap in my life, and in a perverse way, this guilt serves to justify the suffering I deserve. What a crock of waste product! Yet guilt is so deeply ingrained into the human psyche that it is virtually a default program for unawakened humanity. At the root of guilt is our belief in sin, the arrogant notion that we could do anything that could alter reality and change the changeless.

When you consider that unconscious guilt is at the root of all our projections of separation and thus our own suffering, it behooves you to immediately dispel this pernicious illusion; the sooner the better! Considering that all illness, disease, and death is caused by unconscious guilt and belief in the need for sacrifice to "atone for our sins," should we not begin to dissolve this pointless pollution at its source?

The source of this deep, unconscious, or what I call ontological guilt (guilt for simply existing) is our collective belief that somehow our dream-desire for the separation experience actually happened, and in doing so we not only deeply offended God, but we actually destroyed perfection. In short, we believe that God is really, really disappointed and angry at us for what we thought we did!

Our belief in guilt is entirely wrapped up with our belief in sin. Surely we must have done the unforgivable if God is so angry! How convenient that we can project our guilt and belief in sin onto others, and by "sacrificing" them (punish, kill, imprison, wage war), we can get the Big Guy off our backs for a while.

We can feel safe in our isolation if we decide to punish God by denying his existence at all. Of course the joke is on the ego, as we only affirm what we reject by making it real first, then pretending it's not. The absurdity of our fantasies can seem funny at times. The Course even states that we got into this pickle of separation by forgetting to laugh at the notion as it first appeared in our mind.

Many who consider themselves atheists are inadvertently waking up to the preposterous notion of a dualistic god as promulgated by mainstream religions, particularly the "big three:" Judaism, Christianity, and Islam. I can't blame them for rejecting a god portrayed as paranoid, mean, and angry, with a list of preferred "enemies" (not to mention a serious list of do's and don'ts). Sadly, atheists may not realize that in justifiably rejecting a false god of duality, they mistakenly throw out the real God, just as the early scientists did in the modern era. Then they are left with only the cold comfort of their ego and intellect. No worries. There are no atheists on the deathbed, and all mistakes are already healed and forgiven.

By blame and projection, we think we're in the clear and do not realize that "I only ever experience myself." We didn't *really* get rid of our guilt; we just fooled ourselves and put it off by placing it elsewhere, and in the process our world got smaller and more painful. Like all the ego's plans, this one too is "lose-lose."

Let's set the record straight. Not only does the Big Guy not "hate" us, but the Divine has no knowledge of anything *but* its own completely loving and perfect Beingness and Creation. As that Creation, we can only ever be an extension of that perfection. How could perfection harbor or even imagine illusion? Western cultures have projected onto the Divine an image of our own schizophrenic state of mind. We have projected an image of an all-too-human anthropomorphic god as angry and outside of us, like an aloof patriarch who has learned to communicate only through anger. Thus we see God as capable of the insane things we do, including propagating the bane of divisive tribalism in the form of modern nationalism, justifiably hating his enemies, and sending "his wrath." Excuse me? What happened to love?

Further, to add drama to the drama, humans have been historically taken advantage of by non-Earthly beings masquerading as gods. This is a fact of history only recently uncovered, and not yet accepted into the mainstream. I refer you to the works of Zecheria Sitchin and Neil Freer in this regard. The gods of which I speak were more accurately "enslavers" of mankind who gave credence to the popular religious image of an angry male God. I gave much attention to this topic in my first book, so I will not repeat the story here. Suffice to say that in their colonization of Earth, the bullies on the Galactic block left a legacy of fear and intimidation, characteristics that unfortunately have been absorbed by many modern believers in the ancient tribal and dualistic religions established by these counterfeit "gods" even today.

I think you will agree that it is time to let the ancient gods go back to where they came from . . . out of the mists of our unconscious fears based simply on errors in perception. Whatever purpose they may have served in the past is no longer needed. We do not need spiritual "masters" or to remain spiritual "slaves" to outmoded dualistic thought systems. The scaffolding of ancient beliefs have become our prison bars. Let them fall of their own accord, as they are based on nothing real, and certainly not the love they espouse.

Much will change in our world when all illusions within us ultimately dissolve. The false walls that separate us will cease to exist. Borders will be anachronisms. Disputes will be resolved through the willing investigation of the illusions they represent, not on which side "wins" or is "right." The idea of unforgivable sins will be replaced with a sense of compassionate justice, recognizing that where fear once reigned, we can allow love to bloom. Forgiveness will be appreciated as a true "science of healing" and all illness and suffering will be recognized as originating in the mind.

Recognizing guilt as the biggest con game in the Universe will be instrumental to the dismantling of ego-based systems and institutions. We now understand that guilt is not reality-based, but rather based on the illusion of separation. Guilt is the result of a mistake, not a reality, and mistakes can be corrected. Because separation is only a belief and not a fact, there is no real basis for guilt. Does this mean you and I are perfect, innocent, and invulnerable beings of Light right now? Yes, as far as our reality goes. *This life,* therefore, must not be reality. In truth, there is no dream of separation, only a dreamer who thinks there is.

Another thing we can commit to in the time we have in Earth School is choosing positive, loving, and supportive thoughts to replace the old, conditioned programs. After all, we will continue to think for a while yet (I think!). This is one reason why I am eternally grateful to have the Course in my life. For me, this monumental work offers a lifetime's worth of beautiful, uplifting, and most importantly, non-dual thoughts that never fail to remind me of the truth of my being, bringing me consistently to the feeling of peace. We do need to thoroughly clean out the closets of our minds, but we also need to replace what we've removed as long as we think that we think.

When I look back to the most positive turning points in my life, I see that there was always some kind of realization that went along with the events—a realization that "stuck" because I resonated with it in truly recognizing it's timeless value. I call these understandings "thoughts of God" because they seem to point in that direction. Not that I think God has "thoughts" in the ordinary sense. Non-dual thoughts can, however, lead us above the clouds of illusion and open us up to new vistas of hope and healing. They are like Divine prescriptions from the hand of someone who knows exactly what you need and what is best for you now. Divine thoughts are the lifeline Creator offers you even as you dream you are here. They carry the vibration of perfection as pointers to *that which is beyond all thought.*

By systematically "catching" and correcting our misperceptions and consciously choosing more loving and forgiving thoughts, we can begin to add wind to the sails of our wholly minds, collapse time, and become more effective at positively influencing others and the world. Non-dual works like ACIM, the Vedas, and the Tao provide perceptual tools that serve to heal the mind of the symptoms of separation and speed the recovery of the mind back to its original state of Oneness with Source.

Some have said that the Course has more in common with Buddhism than it does with modern Christianity, and I would agree. Buddhism, like the Course, points to the importance of recognizing the mind as "the level of cause," and thus the most effective area in which to effect change. Religions that are caught up in the right vs. wrong game are clearly reflective of a dualistic or separated state of mind. Dualistic religions fall easily under the sway of dualistic politics and economies, and easily become the philosophical arm of dysfunctional and divisive powers. Most sadly, they misrepresent Creator and create further separation by using guilt, exclusivity, sacrifice, and suffering as purported paths to salvation.

Buddhism is generally representative of Eastern thought, which, like the cultures of the Eastern hemisphere of the globe and the right hemisphere of your brain, is *yin* or feminine in its operation and orientation. By *yin* I also mean that the Eastern cultures are typically more group-oriented than individualist. Large populations living with limited resources find that cooperation is a necessary survival tactic and individualism a luxury few can afford. One criticism of the Eastern path is that it leaves out God in the sense of a single, loving Source of all true Creation. Instead, the goal of Eastern practices is to discover the Oneness inherent in particular states of consciousness, among these the peace achieved through realization of non-duality.

The Judeo-Christian traditions, which include Islam, are more *yang* in character, being more individualist, proactive in worldly affairs, and essentially skewed toward male dominance, like your brain's left hemisphere and the cultures of the Western world. I am speaking generalities here, but the themes are compelling.

With the Course, we have a unique marriage of Buddhist non-dualism and the Western concept of a single, unified, and loving Creator. Just as self-actualization or enlightenment entails a joining of mind functions into a unified "whole brain" state, the Course offers the world a synthesis of philosophies that can help guide us toward a unified future: one world recognizing a transcendent non-dual God, free from all conflict, war, and hatred. Again, do we really have a choice?

Non-dual thoughts can help to undo and override the illusion of separation in the mind, as there is no real argument, debate, or conflict with reality and truth. Nothing outside of truth is true (or real, for that matter). Correcting perception heals the mind of the cause of suffering, illness, and pain. Corrected thoughts in themselves can only be pointers to non-dual truth, as Eckhart Tolle reminds us. A non-dual truth is a reminder of who you are in reality, as One who never left the side of perfection, and who in truth remains there. Allow non-dual truths to be felt as much as heard. This is important because these truths point to a state of being beyond the "split" mind—beyond analysis (equal to paralysis) or dissection. The peaceful feeling that comes as we open to new octaves of understanding *will lead to knowledge* of unshakable and irreversible reality.

One of the "cosmic jokes" we have played on ourselves but have not quite yet "gotten" is that the awakening process is so much easier and natural than staying asleep. It takes a lot of effort and dedication to keep up the charade of separation and illusion. Because we have adapted to our limitations, it appears that the stress of illusions is a natural, normal part of existence. We maintain our illusions through our thoughts, which are also judgments against ourselves. Judgment is hard work. Because it is divisive and never fully coherent or integrated with our wholeness, once we start on the path of judgment, we are resigned to a hard road with many rocks and potholes to dodge. Releasing others and ourselves through forgiveness is the end of that struggle and effort.

Think of the panic of a lost child who worries, "If Mommy and Daddy don't find me, I'm gonna die! How will I survive? How will I eat? Where will I live?" All that painful effort at finding solutions is immediately replaced by feelings of love and safety the moment we glimpse Mommy or Daddy standing there with open arms. All that suffering and our imagined future of endless loneliness and separation are gone in an instant of recognition!

They say the smartest thing to do when you get lost in the wilderness is to sit still and wait for someone to find you. This takes a lot less effort, conserves your energy, and will more likely bring the whole drama to a much swifter end. Get the analogy? Give up the struggle with the image on the screen. Relax back into the mind that is causing your experiences, and accept the gift of healing you were given the moment the mind lapsed into unconsciousness. Because of its inherent impossibility, the Universe of separation and suffering was truly over the moment it was imagined. We are living in "the impossible dream" and although it appears you are "in" the dream, in fact you are, as the Course puts it, "safe at home while dreaming of exile."

CONTEMPLATION

Allow these thoughts to take you to a place of peace within.

Create the Inner Sanctuary and learn from the Inner Teacher who only speaks in the silence. Your breath will help you stay focused until the feeling of Oneness and re-union itself pulls you completely within its loving embrace.

Let go of all the thoughts, feelings, and grievances that attempt to keep you unaware of this Peace. Surrender them and then yourself to the Light. Breathing in your own resistance in the form of what you no longer want on the in-breath and accepting the newness of what you do want on the out-breath is a very powerful practice.

Do not be content with concepts only. Honor them and use them, but only to take you to the place within where the Divine Spark dwells. Feeling provides a much better roadmap to our destination than thinking. This is the inner compass that will guide you home.

NINE

Recognizing Reality

Now we will begin to focus on the importance of relationships. In the modern world, we have become further and further isolated from each other because of our belief that we need to become, through our own efforts, autonomous beings, rugged individuals who stand on their own two feet and have conquered the world through sweat and struggle.

The modern market-driven philosophy of narcissism is a complete denial of and totally antithetical to the fact of Oneness. We cannot thrive as separate beings because we are *not* separate beings! Let's get over it! Although you may not yet believe it, *there is only One of us here!* We cannot "figure things out" on our own because we only truly exist in relationship with each other; with Nature; and most importantly, with our only true reality, our Source. Without these interrelated aspects of life, we do not exist at all. Without the lie of separation, there is no basis for a thought-made imaginary self or ego whatsoever.

We like to think of ourselves as autonomous beings, yet your body alone represents at least fifty trillion potentially autonomous cells that have agreed to become One on your behalf. In *The Global Brain Awakens*, Peter Russell likens humans on the planet to a collection of neurons on the verge of firing up as a unified being.[9] We are opening up to the next phase of human evolution as we shed the skin of our separate existence. In *Spontaneous Evolution*, Bruce Lipton identified humanity as being at the same cyclic jump point that single-cell organisms made eons ago when they spontaneously "got it" and the world witnessed an explosion in multi-cellular plants and animals.[10] A whole new order showed up virtually overnight. In his works including *The Third Millennium*, Ken Carey channeled the same story, relaying how we are in a phase shift from an age of individual awakening to the emergence of a single, unified Planetary Being.[11] In the timeless holographic Universe, there is nothing new under the Sun.

Decades ago the philosopher Arthur Koestler conceived the concept of the Holon. This was the idea that the

....

9. Peter Russell, *The Global Brain Awakens: Our Next Evolutionary Leap* (Palo Alto, CA: Global Brain Inc., 1995).

10. Bruce H. Lipton, Steve Bhaerman, *Spontaneous Evolution: Our Positive Future* (Carlsbad, CA: Hay House, 2009).

11. Ken Carey, *The Third Millennium: Living in the Posthistoric World* (San Francisco, CA: Harper San Francisco, 1991).

Universe is made up of seemingly individual units of wholeness that combine to create a larger, unified wholeness. Anything that could be conceived of as a self-contained unit, starting with the atom, could be said to be simultaneously part of a larger unit. From the atom to the molecule to the chemical compound to the organic structures (amino acids) to single-cell organisms, we inhabit a Universe of nested Holons—miniature "wholenesses" holographically resting within a grand unified Oneness.

Imagine that one of your cells decides it is no longer part of a collective, and strikes out on its own to conquer the world. In its madness, it imagines its own rules and purpose, setting about to destroy all that challenge its illusion of specialness, even if it ends up destroying the very body that gave it life to begin with. We have a name for this syndrome. It is called cancer.

We need to begin to dismantle our dysfunctional thoughts and beliefs about ourselves as isolated, separate beings. And where do these thoughts and beliefs most consistently show up? That's right—in our relationships! In the meeting of minds, where relationships are truly experienced, we learn what our own prejudices, fears, and unconscious guilt patterns truly are. Why do over half of modern marriages dissolve into painful separations? Could it be that those entering these contracts on the level of ego or personality have *no idea* what "relationship" actually entails?

Relationships can be difficult to think about, as we are so often focused on the *individuals* in relationships, and their needs and perceptions. "Relationship" can seem like a vague notion that describes the space between two things without a specific concrete object or focus of attention. Many turn their backs on understanding relationships when they get to the point where they can't think straight about them. Rather than focus on the individuals in the relationship, we could look at the larger Holon of the relationship itself. From the ego's limited point of view, we typically look at the need for one or the other to change somehow in order for the relationship to become harmonious. Typically, we reason that if something about the other person could change, then the relationship could be harmonious. This is because the ego functions by isolating specifics rather than yielding to a more abstract awareness of the relationship as a unit. Being wrapped up in the details of the situation, the ego loses sight of the larger principle at work. We become distracted by the behaviors, perceptions, judgments, and fears that are driving our felt need for conflict. Been there, done that. Because of all the conflicting energies running through our minds, the notion of "working on this relationship" can seem daunting, if not hopeless. Be assured the ego does not seek true solutions; rather its credo is always "divide and conquer."

A helpful learning aid for me in this area arrived in the form of my understanding of sacred geometry. Geometries provide the blueprints of Creation. From a metaphysical perspective, they provide the energetic templates for the formation of matter from the even subtler realms of light and sound. Geometries are seen in the repeating patterns we observe in nature, and are part of the "architecture of matter" in the Universe. According to Barbara Hand Clow's nine-dimensional model, sacred geometry and mathematics are the sixth dimension—a dimension that translates sacred sound and light (7D and 8D) into form. 6D provides the organizational blueprints for the manifestation of energy into matter. In his seminal work *The Fields of Life*, Dr. Harold Saxon Burr of Yale University proposed that the measurable energy fields around plant seeds contain all the information for the development of that seed into a full adult life form. The implication is that this field, what we are describing as a 6D informational template, is the blueprint not only for growth, but for the regeneration (healing) of that organism in the face of illness or injury.[12]

Sacred geometries can help us understand and visualize how things "down here" in the physical world are structured—even intangible things like morphogenic fields, belief systems held in collective consciousness, and relationships. Within the geometry of relationship, we learn how our relationships were originally formed and see how they became unbalanced and frustrating. We also find a roadmap within these geometries for the healing ("becoming whole") of these relationships.

In simplest of terms, the first form in sacred geometry, the circle, symbolizes the totality of Source as perfect and harmonized within itself. The circle is, of course,

....

12. Harold Saxon Burr, *The Fields of Life: Our Links with the Universe* (New York: Ballantine, 1973).

a two-dimensional representation of a sphere; I find the sphere to be a more accurate model of description for our purposes. The circle as an image only represents the idea of All That Is in a self-contained yet infinite state of pure creative being. Trying to describe the One Source is frustrating because it is impossible, as we already determined. The "unlimited" cannot be limited to a concept, or even a sophisticated set of concepts. Even the symbol of the circle is deceptive in that the edge of the circle implies boundaries, and the Divine has none! So, given how our minds operate, the circle is more a symbol for us; it shows us how our limited understanding causes us to put boundaries around anything before we think we can understand it.

But for now, the circle works. The second symbol arising within sacred geometry describes the separation of one equal circle from the first:

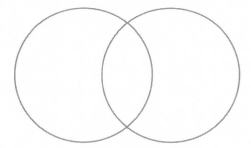

This event or movement away from the state of Oneness symbolizes the apparent effect of the "crazy mad idea" of separation that arose within the first circle (as described in our section on metaphysical premises). It is hard to imagine why or how this question arose, but it did. Maybe it was inevitable that the question of separation would come up, as within the original perfect circle, all ideas are permissible, possible, and thus eventually probable. Inevitably, the idea of the "opposite" of perfect Oneness had to be allowed in order to be lived, processed, and learned from. What are we learning from the seeming state of separation? That separation does not work because it is not really possible!

Notice, though, that the second circle (for me, that's the one that moved to the right, although it doesn't really matter how you see it) did not leave the first completely. It only stuck one foot out of the first circle, keeping the other firmly rooted in its Source. This elegantly describes how our illusion of separation, which started (in this Universe at least) with the Big Bang, in fact did not *really* happen—it was impossible. The illusion "happened" only in our mind (we are the One who chose to test the idea of separation) in the sense that we bought into our desired experience. All our attention was drawn into the dream-Universe and we conveniently forgot that the other foot never left home at all.

A good way to think of this mass self-deception is that we fell asleep under a spell of our own desire. Now, if this is the case, we must be a pretty darn powerful creative being! And that is exactly so. We—that is, the collective mind containing all that is in this Universe, both animate and inanimate—are the One True Creation, the

One True Self of All That Truly Is. We existed as such before the Universe in a state of pure Oneness with our Creator within the perfect circle-sphere of Oneness. This is still the reality of our True Being. The Course refers to us as the "Sonship" . . . the unified One offspring of the Divine. In this sense, there is only One Creator and One Creation. The rest is a figment of our "split mind." This One Creation is the Son of God Jesus talked about . . . not about himself as a special human, but about his realization that he and all of us are of the same Source, and are forever joined in that Unified Being. "I and my Father are One" is a statement of non-duality rather than "specialness," wherein there is no separation between Creator and Creation. No exceptions. Oneness therefore includes you. Ultimately, even the separation between God and God's Creation dissolves, and all we are left with is the realization that "God is." This statement is the closest any mind can come to in conceiving ultimate reality, and as such is a wonderful mantra for meditation.

The "overlap" between Source and us in our imagined separation forms a perfect geometric shape known as the *vesica pisces*. It is a shape we see reflected throughout Creation, perhaps as a reminder that we are forever joined with Source. It is the geometry of the shape of your eye, for example. This overlap between the circles represents the part of you that never left your Source. This is your Divine Self, aware of its own source and knowing that part of you has forgotten your Source and is "lost in space" in its own dream/nightmare of separation. You could say the vesica pisces represents your "right mind" that is still safe at home, while your "wrong mind" is flailing out in space and time trying to make sense of a hallucination.

As electromagnetic theorist James Maxwell suggested more than a century ago, there are ranges of energy that we cannot perceive or measure.[13] Maxwell called these energies *hyper-spatial dimensions,* as he recognized that the ranges of energy transcended our normal limits of measurable time and space. These more esoteric aspects of electromagnetism were written out of Maxwell's work, as it is taught in university-level courses to this day.

Later, Colonel Tom Beardon coined the phrase *scalar wave* to describe these unique energies. It turns out that an energetic portal into non-physical dimensions is created at the intersection of two equal but oppositely charged electromagnetic fields. On first glance it would appear that the two overlapping fields cancel each other out, but this is only partially true. Nature abhors a vacuum, and *something* has to happen in the neutral space that is created at this intersection of fields. This "portal," for lack of a better term, creates an access point to ranges of energy that are usually beyond our ability to perceive or measure. This is why mainstream materialist science has difficulty with these ideas, as what is immeasurable to science is not only invisible; it does not exist. Do I sense a massive conspiracy of denial of the "unseen" here? And who could be afraid

....

13. James Clerk Maxwell, *A Dynamical Theory of the Electromagnetic Field* (London: Royal Society of London, 1864).

of the truth of anything beyond materialism? Only ego, of course.

The energies implied by scalar openings include, but are not limited to, psychic potentials such as telepathy, "seeing" possible futures, and even such outlandish possibilities as teleportation and transmutation. These potentials operate according to known quantum principles, including non-locality and indeterminacy. Although these and other quantum principles are based on "bedrock" scientific validation, because they do not apply directly to the physical dimensions ruled by our senses, they still seem fantastical to the linear mind. Technologies that employ scalar energy do exist, and are kept largely under wraps by the prevailing power structures. They will inevitably come forward. They include the high potential for "free energy" systems, ultimately releasing us from the chains of corporate monopolies and their money/oil addiction.

The fact that this electromagnetic model mirrors the geometry of Creation speaks to the holographic nature of this Universe. It is as if we left clues or breadcrumbs throughout our Creation to give ourselves opportunities to find our way home.

Consider another implication of the dual circle symbol. Let's say the left circle represents your brain's left hemisphere and its electromagnetic signature field, and the right circle represents your right hemisphere. We all know the brain and nervous system are partially electrical. The brain produces clear and measurable electromagnetic field effects, known in biofeedback to produce EEG readings.

If we consider the left hemisphere in its linear and logical functioning to operate in a yang state, and the right hemisphere in its global and non-verbal intelligence to operate in a yin state, we could say we have represented two equal but oppositely charged electromagnetic fields with a point of intersection connecting them.

I find it interesting that in the middle of your brain at the point of energetic intersection of your hemispheres there is a vestigial "eye" looking upward in the form of the pineal gland. Many feel that enlightenment is to some degree associated with the activation of the pineal gland in the role of the 3D eye, the eye of wisdom associated with the Brow Chakra and Inner Vision. Apparently this gland has the same rods and cones, or specialized light sensors, as do your two physical eyes. Is it our destiny to evolve from the "two-eyed" human entrapped within dualistic perception to the "awakened" human who sees reality through the One Eye of the Unified Mind, supported in this function by the scalar field generated within the brain?

Another of the gifts of this symbol is that it reminds us that no matter what we experience in the dream of separation, who we truly are is not affected. We are invulnerable beings pretending to be vulnerable. We are Spiritual Beings at One with our Source entertaining an outlandish fantasy as we "play" within our creative potential. If the growth trajectory of a human life is any reflection of our reality, can we expect that we will soon tire of child's play, and begin to recognize the inner urge to grow up and begin to use our creative potential outside the sandbox of our childish fantasies? Perhaps we don't have a choice. The sun is setting, dinner's on the table, and our loving parent is calling us to abandon our playing and come home.

In a practical sense, you can use the image of the two circles to appreciate and relate to the sense of common ground in your one-to-one relationships. Know that each person in a relationship is operating in one of two possible modes. If they are in their "outside mode"; that is, thinking they are outside of the Oneness that created them, then they will relate to you through the "two eyes" of duality and ego—the belief that you are two entirely separate beings. If, however, you decide to join with that person in your recognition of the "overlap", that is, the commonality of Spirit that joins all relationships in Creation, then you will be operating from your Spirit or your memory of your Divine Source. It will be much easier for you to overlook (literally forgive) the ego/mind with which you are engaged when you realize you are talking to an idea held within a Divine, albeit sleeping mind equally at One with you and your Source.

To actually do this is not as hard as you may think. It only requires the willingness to ask. Simply say to yourself just before or as you engage with another, "Spirit (or God or Jesus or Allah or however you conceive of Spirit), I want you to be present as I engage this person. Help me see You and the One Self we all share behind their words and actions. I celebrate your Presence and Thank you for this person . . . who I recognize is another Me."

I love the word "recognize." If you think of it as meaning to "re-cognize," the implication is that we are remembering what we must have known at one time, but have forgotten. "Help me to re-cognize that we are the One Creation in a state of temporary amnesia."

According to the basics of sacred geometry, the next division was when the circles became three, then more, and kept exponentially dividing until we have a separate circle representative of every part of the Universe of form. That pattern of expanding form is replicated every time a human being is conceived and develops from one cell to ultimately trillions. It doesn't matter if the form is a galaxy or a subatomic particle—that form is held within the body of "nested circles" or interconnected energy fields, each one connected to every other form through the overlaps that remain at every level. The idea of an interconnected matrix of Holons, going back to Koestler, gave rise to holographic theory, a theory based on the observation of how in a holographic image, every infinitesimal part of the image carries all of the information held by the whole. By this theory, each individual human remains a complete "image" of its Creator . . . we are "made in his/her image."

I am reminded of one of my favorite quotes from Golas's *Lazy Man's Guide to Enlightenment:* "We are all equal beings, and the Universe is our relationships with each other."[14] Think of any part of the Universe—the person sitting next to you, or a star on the other side of the galaxy. You are connected by the "web of life" to that thing. The Course says that "All thought produces form on some level." From this, we may assume that all form originates from thought. The fact that you could think of anything means that you and that thing are already connected on some level within the One Mind. Otherwise, it could not be a part of your movie.

Scientists are bumping up against the same conclusion, referring to the ultimate Oneness of all objects and energy fields as "quantum entanglement." They are beginning to see the essential unity of the dream but as yet have not acknowledged its illusory nature or the need for a Creator or Dreamer.

The notion of the interconnected matrix of Creation (*matrix* is the Latin root for "mother" as well as "material" and "matter") is perfectly illustrated in the symbol of the Flower of Life. There are a few other recognized subdivisions of this geometric form, and to understand them we would need an in-depth look at sacred geometry. Others have already covered much of this material, so we will not do so here. The Flower of Life, though, merits a closer look.

....
14. Thaddeus Golas, *The Lazy Man's Guide to Enlightenment* (Layton, Utah: Gibbs Smith, 1972).

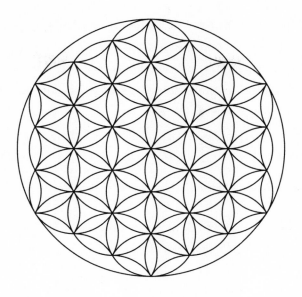

The Flower of Life is found all over the world embedded in architecture, ancient writings, ceramic tiles, statues, and art. It represents the completion of the original separation into all the various forms of matter. Within the image are embedded the five Platonic Solids, which provide the structural blueprints for all matter. If you soften your gaze as you look at the Flower of Life, you may be able to discern some of them. All natural structures from the micro to the macro are supported by one of these forms. In his recent work *The Source Field Investigations*, David Wilcock points out that even the positions of planets, stars, and galaxies in space are determined by these energetic templates.[15] The Earth herself is nested in geometries

15. David Wilcock, *The Source Field Investigations* (New York: Dutton, 2011).

that appear in the form of ley lines and energy vortexes or "power places," where the natural energies that flow along geometric lines concentrate. Following are the five Platonic Solids all contained in the Flower of Life.

| Tetrahedron | Hexahedron | Octahedron | Dodecahedron | Icosahedron |

With this brief look at the geometries of Creation we come back to the idea that the "map" works in two directions. One direction points to expansion, the development of life forms, and further separation. The second direction serves as a roadmap home. This map provides clues about how to recognize the constructs of separation, and through will and intention, use this knowledge to "deconstruct" the dream universe and ultimately come back to the point before we fell asleep and where we still remain as Spirit. The "key" to deconstructing our separateness seems to be in the relationships, or "overlaps" of the various forms found within any relationship, no matter how obscure or far out in the matrix they may appear to be. The forms of Creation represent separation and division, while the overlaps represent the common Source of all. The kicker is that *any relationship* offers the same portal home. Even relationships that only exist in our memories can serve this goal, once we decide that healing or becoming whole is our purpose and direction.

Healing all relationships is clearly a massive task. Luckily, the Divine Source knew it would be highly daunting for any person dreaming they were a small and ineffectual individual to even consider the task. Thus we were provided a simple means for fulfilling the job of returning the Creation to the Creator. This means has been called the Divine Messenger, the Inner Healer, the One Self or "Big Mind" of Buddhism, and the Holy Spirit (Whole Spirit) in the Western tradition. It is the all-seeing, all-knowing aspect of the Divine sent into our dream to find us and point the way out. I will use the abbreviation HS to describe this Divine agent.

The HS knows the entire map from beginning to end. The HS is not limited as we are by "split minds" to things like linear logic, a belief in cause and effect, or time. The HS is ever ready to respond to even our slightest desire to awaken, and will turn the entire Universe in your direction to do so. And the HS *cannot fail* in its mission. It sees the end result from the start of this grand experiment in cosmic snoozing, and has no doubt whatsoever that you will make it! If we are a yo-yo spinning out in the Universe at the end of our tether with no particular direction home, then the HS is the string that keeps us connected with Source and eventually will bring us home, perhaps with just a simple jerk of its figurative wrist!

The Divine Messenger, or "comforter," as Jesus referred to it in the Gospels, is an active aspect of Creator sent to find us in the dream and enable us to awaken and return to sanity and the fullness of our true nature. The Divine

Messenger provides a bridge between the lunatic imaginings of the separated mind and the abstract, somewhat foreign sense of a Prime Creator that is beyond our imagination, other than in the symbols of God we have made for ourselves. The HS, like us, has a foot in both reality and illusion, and thus understands our predicament. It also "sees" the entire plan of our awakening from beginning to end, and is always there to assist when we ask. Why not ask the Divine Messenger to come to you in a manner you can accept, and see what happens?

TEN

Forgiving for Good

We have been given the method of forgiveness in order to manifest the idea of returning home by recognizing patterns of separation in our relationships and connection and then re-purposing those relationships. I encourage you to be open to the possibility that there is *nothing* beyond the reach of True Forgiveness—yes, even *that thing* that has been with you so long that it feels like a part of you. Believe it or not, freedom from all suffering is your birthright. Why not decide now that you are not going to let anything stop you from accepting this truth and knowing it for yourself? Decide to ignore the niggling little voices in your head that tell you that you or someone you love is beyond forgiveness' loving embrace, because that is simply *not true!*

How do I know this? The only way anyone can truly know anything: from my own experience. I have experienced the pain of chronic guilt, burning like an ember in the pit of my stomach. I have also experienced the release and joy that follows upon the offering and acceptance of True Forgiveness. I know I am not "special" in this regard. Forgiveness is as free as the wind, as available as sunlight, and much more "real" than the thoughts and beliefs that keep us in suffering. This is because forgiveness is based on the truth of who we are, while guilt, pain, and suffering are only based on an erroneous idea of who we are.

Did you notice that I used the term "True" Forgiveness? Does this mean there is a "false" version of forgiveness? Indeed it does. How do you know when forgiveness is false? Simply, it doesn't work. False forgiveness is like cheap paint. It may cover over a blemish, but when it dries, you still see the problem behind it! In other words, false forgiveness still carries with it an element of guilt, shame, and regret. You've simply traded your ball and chain for one slightly less heavy.

You do not need to settle for anything less than complete and absolute forgiveness, leaving you with nothing but infinite gratitude, self-love, and appreciation. If you are willing to read this work in its entirety and put into practice the simple ideas presented here, you *will* experience for yourself the joy, freedom, and peace that True Forgiveness offers anyone and everyone willing to receive it. No exceptions. In truth, the forgiveness we want is already given. We just need to be ready to receive it.

In order to present a complete picture of True Forgiveness, first we will discuss what forgiveness is *not*. It will be necessary to build a metaphysical context for the full understanding of True Forgiveness. Without this metaphysical context, some of which we have already presented, it would be impossible to grasp and thereby fully experience the freedom we lay claim to. Many of the ideas I will present will fly in the face of "conventional wisdom," especially in the face of limiting religious dogma and tiresome tradition.

You may be curious as to why the kind of forgiveness offered in many religious contexts has not seemed to impact the world very much. Wars and conflicts, many based on religious divisions, continue to plague us, both on the global and personal levels, as we pay lip service to wishes for world peace while singing "Joy to the World" every December like clockwork. We've had two thousand years to practice "Love thy neighbor and forgive your enemies" with the sad result that well over ten million of us perished in the horrendous wars of the twentieth century alone. Clearly a message of forgiveness from the pulpit is not getting through. Forgiveness is not merely a moral obligation or merely wishful thinking. Forgiveness is the way home and the path that all sincere awakeners will eventually find on their own healing journey.

We are in a whole lot of trouble here if we don't figure out the true meaning of forgiveness. We must find the means of peace within ourselves if we are to survive and transcend the dubious destructive doctrine of "endless war" on ourselves, each other, and our Earthly home.

As with any topic of such importance, it is well worth the investment of time and energy to step back and attempt to create a larger context with which to view the problem. Trying to solve a problem from the same state of mind that made the problem in the first place is a formula for total failure, as both Einstein and the Maharishi have reminded us. To be clear, the state of mind that thinks it needs forgiveness in the first place is a mistaken state of mind, based on false premises. This is not to say that forgiveness is not helpful as it applies to the dream world of ego and separation. Forgiveness is the undoing of that false world, and it simply represents the means for correction of a fundamental misperception. Once corrected, errors are no more real than a passing thought—they are considered and dismissed as meaningless. This will become clearer to us as we develop new lines of thinking. We need to explore the false premises that convince us we are beyond forgiveness, and decide for ourselves to put them aside.

We are not reaching for the moon here—we are referring to a systematic process of "unlearning" while taking on an entirely new perspective. Stated otherwise, when we remove the blinders, it's much easier to see what is already there. The blinders we want to remove are those of guilt, shame, condemnation, judgment, and the belief in "sin" or the inherent imperfection of ourselves and humankind. Although it may seem like these negative qualities are just part of being human, they are much more like a false background that you might see in an amateur stage play. In the context of the fantasy within the play, these props appear to represent reality. But when the show is over and everybody goes home, we see the props for what they are: skillfully made illusions.

How did we get to the point where we could accept these shallow falsehoods as truth? What set us on this course of guilt and shame that underlies all of our misbehavior toward ourselves and each other? If we can untie this knot in our minds, will we be free to discover a true foundation for recovering our original nature as pure, loving, and compassionate beings? Are you willing to find out?

ELEVEN

The Cost of Not Forgiving

Dr. Ryke Geerd Hamer of Germany has made one of the most amazing discoveries regarding the cause and cure for cancer. We don't generally know about Dr. Hamer's work because he was vilified, victimized, and hounded (all by "legal" means, of course) for having discovered a cure for cancer that did not fall within the narrow paradigm of the modern drugs and surgery medical mafioso model. That's right, folks. Do you want a firsthand look at the self-righteous viciousness of the military-industrial-petro-chemical-medical cartel? Just discover and publicize a "cure for cancer" and you'll find out quickly! Cancer, like other major degenerative diseases today, is Big Business. As of this writing, we do not have a medical health care system in the developed world. We have a highly profitable and woefully inadequate disease care system that is entrenched in an outmoded materialist paradigm that the rest of modern science has long since moved beyond. The mounting death statistics from cancer and other degenerative (life-style-based) diseases are part of the price we pay for the lack of forgiveness. For more information on Dr. Hamer and the book, *The German New Medicine,* visit *www.new-medicine.ca.*

Dr. Hamer was a practicing physician in a large German hospital. One of his jobs was to administer and read brain scans. His "new medicine" was the result of seeing thousands of brain scans and making certain observations. Something that caught Dr. Hamer's attention was the occasional appearance of distortions in the scan images that looked like patterns you would see when you dropped a pebble into a clear pond: concentric circles radiating out from a center point, like a target. At first he assumed that there was something wrong with the equipment, perhaps picking up on some exogenous interference. When Hamer asked the manufacturer of the brain scan equipment if these patterns could indicate a flaw or environmental disturbance, the equipment manufacturer assured him that if the patterns were showing up in the brain scan images, then they were definitely showing something that was occurring in the patient's brain. They could not be the product of some outside interference.

Ever the curious scientist, Hamer noted that these patterns only appeared in patients who either had a diagnosed cancer, or would be diagnosed with cancer within six months of the scan! He set about doing an epidemiological study, basically checking in with a lot of patients over time, and came up with some other significant correlations. Specifically, Hamer noted that the location of the "energetic lesion," as he called it, in the brain was correlated with the location or organ in the body where the cancer was or would soon manifest. As he interviewed these patients, he found a further correlation between the location of the brain scan pattern, the location and type of cancer, and a commonly held emotional memory or unresolved emotional conflict in the life of the patient.

In the patients who were able to recognize the emotional conflict at the root of the pattern *and resolve the conflict through recognizing their innocence and mistaken self-blame and guilt*, not only did the pattern in the scan resolve itself (disappear), but so did the cancer. Thousands of case studies proved beyond any reasonable doubt that cancer can be cured by a change in one's thinking! The medical name for a healing not attributable to medical intervention is a "spontaneous remission." Medical blindness often pushes aside "miraculous" healings with pompous assertions like "the chemo must have worked!" or "the diagnosis must have been wrong!" just to save face. We can't have miracles messing with our science! Yet these "miracles" only represented a simple change of perspective in the mind.

If Hamer's work reveals an access point to what the ancients and natural healers of old called the "Inner Healer," would you not think this would be hailed as one of the greatest medical discoveries of all time?

Hamer's research and subsequent theory of healing, which he continued working with despite being hounded and often jailed, could be summarized as follows. When there is a completely unexpected trauma (loss of a loved one, severe accident, divorce, etc.), the conscious mind is challenged to provide meaning in its own defense. The unexpected and irrational nature of these traumas represents a major threat to our psychological survival, or at least that of our self-image—the ego. One job of the conscious mind is to make sense of the changing world around us and enable us to navigate it safely. Yet these anomalous life events have no basis in rationality. They seem to "come out of the blue" like an unwelcomed sucker punch. The mind reels in its attempt to make sense out of the senseless—to make rational the irrational. It does this in order to psychologically survive the trauma with an intact concept of the self (ego).

We also create meaning for our traumatic experiences in our own defense, believing that in doing so we will see the trauma coming next time, and be prepared to avoid it. Giving meaning to our experience is what some say "makes us human" or "conscious, self-reflective beings" rather than beings motivated purely by instinct. The shortfall here is in our assumption that this "self" of which we are conscious is in fact our real Self. It is not. It is a false self, made up to accommodate our belief in our separate existence. Only when we become truly conscious of our true limitless Self as Divine Creation will we be able to claim we are fully alive, or fully "Hu-man" which can be translated as a "sacred man."

The sheer emotional impact of a traumatic event is first registered in the brain non-verbally. It is usually painful, shocking, or upsetting, but as pure primary perception, it is still essentially neutral. It just *is* without judgment. The conscious, verbal ego-mind, however, is not satisfied to just let the experience "be." As noted, it must explain to itself the "why" of the event in order to survive intact and prevent a similar event in the future. This is just how our conscious mind and its attachment to time operates in its fear-based and obsessive need for self-protection and security.

When there is no rational explanation for an event, the mind, in its desperate attempt to make sense out of the senseless, will accept a weak or false explanation rather than no explanation at all. It would rather entertain a deception than admit it has no control over events now or in the future. By default, the mind will gravitate to the deep well of unconscious guilt we all carry within for an answer to its conundrum. This is "ontological guilt" or guilt for simply being alive in a seemingly separate state. This guilt is shared by all humans, and is the deep unconscious scar we carry resulting from our desire for and belief in the idea of separation from our Source. It is the commonly held "Big Bang psychosis."

As our unconscious guilt supplies the "rationale" for the trauma to the satisfaction of the conscious mind and is accepted as the reason for the incident, it becomes "oncological" guilt. The cause of cancer in Hamer's view and in the broadest sense is the unconscious guilt that may actually be the mental-emotional root of all disease.

In the brain scans he worked with, Dr. Hamer saw the electromagnetic signature of what psychologists call "cognitive dissonance." You have one perceptual process going on (the raw perception of the incident before interpretation) overlaid by the conceptual choice of *why* this terrible thing happened. As dictated by guilt, the belief that typically emerges is "It was my fault. If I were just a better (wife, husband, mother, father, boss, employee, whatever . . .), this terrible thing would not have happened. I know I am to blame, and although I feel awful with this burden of well-deserved guilt, at least I know what caused the event, and can now try to move on." Note the ego-satisfying sense of martyrdom here. Sacrifice is a notion deeply wedded to our unconscious belief that we need to somehow "pay for" our unforgivable sins.

The medical system adds to the deception by pronouncing a "diagnosis" and regarding the "patient" as merely a set of symptoms with a statistically bound destiny and guaranteed low survival rate (assuming the patient agrees to their dismally unsuccessful standard treatments). Do you think telling someone "You have six months to live" might not imprint this belief and create a self-fulfilling prophecy, especially if the pronouncement is made by a white-coated demi-god of the academic medical priesthood?

The self-blaming version of the story imposed over the neutral primary perception creates an energetic "lock-up," like two oppositely spinning tornadoes locked in a dance of mutual destruction. This event could be described as electromagnetic cognitive dissonance, a condition that blocks the natural energy flow in the brain and shows up as a distinctive pattern in brain scans.

The part of the brain that this "energy lesion" shows up in is part of a critical communication system. The organ or area of the body reliant on this area of the brain to coordinate and inform it is now cut off—exiled from the greater community of cells and organs. Excommunication is a terrible punishment for both humans and the body itself. The belief in separation that fed the guilt in the first place has now become manifest and solidified in the body. The exiled organ and cells become weak and vulnerable to all kinds of stress and attack, and eventually accept a pattern of disease in order to bring attention to themselves, saying in effect, "Hey, pay attention! Something's 'off' here, and I need you to look into it!" What medicine identifies as causes and risk factors for disease are merely secondary factors or potential predispositions that may never manifest as illness without this emotional level of original cause in place. Why is it that two people exposed to the very same risk factors for a disease have completely different outcomes? The verbal brain looks for and is satisfied with simple cause-and-effect relationships within the limits of its own perceptions without any real evidence they are in any way related.

In the cases where Hamer's patients recognized the irrationality of their self-blaming and guilt over what happened (in some cases, a benefit of time and retrospection) and took themselves 'off the hook' the target pattern in the brain simply dissolved, communication was restored, and healing was experienced. This process was proven in thousands of real case studies. Hamer's work provides an elegant illustration of the principle that the mind creates the body, not the other way around (as is currently held by the scientific religion of materialism). Hopefully, one day soon, Hamer's accomplishment will be recognized and we can get on with the true meaning of healing: "becoming whole" again.

Hamer discovered that it can take from five to twenty years for an unresolved emotional conflict to manifest in the form of diagnosable cancer. He also provided the reasoning for why, after standard "poisons and surgery" cancer therapy, which have no solid statistical research-based validity, that in many cases the cancer returns in about five years, often in a more virulent form. If the cause of disease in the mind is not addressed, the body has no choice but to manifest this cause again even if the diseased tissue is removed.

With standard cancer treatment, you are not considered "cured" until you have been cancer-free for five years following conventional therapy. It is no secret that the barbaric and unscientific approach to cancer in the modern world is more often the cause of death than the disease itself—primarily through the disabling of the immune system. As noted, diagnosis is too often a self-fulfilling prophecy, proving the power of the mind to create based on its own belief. Iatrogenic disease is the official name for "death by medicine" and has been identified as a top killer in our world today.[16]

Sometimes, though, "drugs and surgery" medicine appears to work! Could it be that with or without standard treatment, by recognizing and forgiving (overlooking) the mind's guilt-based beliefs, the root cause of the disease is addressed inadvertently and the patient heals despite the standard therapy? It is likely that being diagnosed with a potentially life-threatening illness can inspire some to become more introspective and reflective on their life patterns, and to realize how they took on guilt groundlessly without a formal process. No cause, no effect! Dr. Hamer's story is just one (albeit concrete) example of how changing our minds changes our bodies and can create miracles of healing. The entire field of mind-body medicine supports this example. But what about the less life-threatening but equally peace-destroying challenges of our lives . . . relationship problems, career issues, addictions? Can these areas and others be as directly affected by a simple change of mind? Let's see how True Forgiveness offers a means to correct every misperception we have ever had about ourselves as mirrored to us in our day-to-day relationships, and how these relationships offer us a road home to the peace, joy, and fullness of being we in truth never left.

....
16. Source: *www.mercola.com.*

TWELVE

It's All in the Mind

Let's look at one of the basic assumptions we tend to accept without question in the modern world: that consciousness, or mind, is the end result of the evolution of matter. Somehow, as this popular belief holds, over eons and quite by cosmic accident, inert matter organized itself into the eventual "crown of Creation" and out of the primordial ooze all the way up the evolutionary ladder to us! That view, the "myth of progress," is still prevalent in academia and conveniently places the academics on top of the heap. Piled high and deep. Our unsubstantiated belief that humanity is the result of the randomness of natural selection requires a lot more faith than does simply accepting that we are an extension of a Divine Creator.

When it was introduced in the mid-1800s, the original theory of evolution offered a refreshing alternative to the notion that we were created by an all-powerful, sometimes-loving, sometimes-murderous and vengeful

God. Darwin's theory as originally proposed in 1846 was in part a reaction to the stifling intellectual atmosphere of the time, as serious thinkers attempted to throw off the heavy veil of historical religious dogma. Not a bad motivation, to be sure! Yet in the process, scientists created a new religion of empirical (measurable) materialism and cultivated a belief in cumulative progress as a basic force of nature. The myopic philosophy of "might makes right", a conclusion in line with Social Darwinism, was one unfortunate offspring of this theory. The theory of evolution as proposed conveniently put the Western (read: white-skinned) colonial powers on top of the hierarchical heap, with every right to exploit and rule over practically everything else in Creation. Here we had the perfect philosophical justification for the age of colonialism, domination, and enslavement.

The philosophy of Social Darwinism extended the notion of adaptation and the survival of the fittest to apply to human social development. The Nazis eventually took this idea of "deserved" mastery to its extreme, as did the Kings of old with their credo of ruling by Divine Right. The natural conclusion in the mind of the modern scientist-priests was that we don't need a "Creator" or a "God"—we evolved quite well without one, thank you. When, however, the evolutionary theorists threw out the bathwater of dogmatic and dualistic religious blindness, they inadvertently tossed out the baby of true human spirituality and substituted one superstition for another.

But what if this "new religion" of scientific rationalism, just like the old one of paternalistic and dualistic religion, was doomed from the start to repeat the patterns of the past and to simply substitute one form of dogmatic belief for another? Why would this be so? The answer is that both science and religion are rooted in the same fundamentally unstable state of mind: that of duality.

Duality, as we have seen, is simply the belief in the co-existence of opposites, which arose naturally out of our desire to experience separation or "twoness" at the dawn of the Creation of the Universe. To recap, this original desire to split off from our home in Oneness set the stage for all suffering by creating the belief and thus perception of the separation of all things into opposite pairs. Everything you perceive or conceive of in the Universe comes in pairs—from subatomic particles to the directions of up and down to qualities of hot and cold, past and future, movement and stillness—all the way up to ontological issues like good and evil. By all appearances, it is apparently a Universe of dualities.

If mind is primary to matter rather than the other way around as Hamer's work suggests, we could then say the entire Universe, including the world we perceive, is the effects, or projections, of this mind. The mind, being currently split between its memory of Oneness and its desire for and belief in separation, would logically project an experience that mirrors this basic dichotomy. Thus the world of duality is only a world of perception, with perception being the result of projection, as the Course states. Look at the physical structure of the human brain—split right down the middle and seeing everything through two eyes! What does that design tell you about the state of our minds?

Psychologists and neuroscientists have learned some surprising things about perception, even from a strictly material viewpoint. First, what we see "out there" is now understood in terms of brain chemistry and functions going on exclusively "in here." Change your brain chemistry and neural connections, and what you perceive "out there" changes. Or consider again the sensory apparatus of an insect. The bug perceives a completely different Universe, yet it is no less "real" to the bug. Because of the split state of mind, what we tend to project out into our world is our own inner conflicted guilt-laden beliefs, thoughts, and wishes. To repeat Deepak Chopra's maxim, "The world is as you are."

Not surprisingly, duality is a "two-edged sword." The downside is that it is a perfect setup for conflict—from the inner arguments we put up with on a day-to-day basis, to the reason why we passionately resist beliefs or ideologies different from ours. We wage war on those things we don't understand or agree with: Communists, Muslims, drugs, poverty, disease . . . the list goes on. Sometimes we see the "opposite" in the future, and so we act in an attempt to balance the future in the present. If I treat you nicely now, you are more likely to not criticize or hurt me in the future. This kind of calculated behavior or bargaining is based on fear, not love.

The "upside" of duality is realized when we give it new purpose. Dealing with opposites offers us the opportunity—the necessity—to make choices. We are constantly choosing between one thing and its opposite, trying to find harmony or balance on the dualistic tightrope. Many of us are making these moment-to-moment choices unconsciously and merely based on past conditioning, beliefs, and self-concepts. Once we realize ("make real") the fact that we are doing this, we can become more conscious or mindful of our choice-making opportunities and begin to awaken our power to create the world we truly want. To revisit an analogy, this is like the horse who goes where he wants while his rider is snoozing, but when the rider wakes up, the "horse" (mind) comes once again under the conscious control of the true decision-maker: you as Spirit.

Exercising choice is much more profound and potentially empowering than it may seem. After all, it was choice that created the Universe as we know it . . . our choice to experience something "other than" or opposite to the state of perfect Oneness. This same power of choice empowered by the activated will can ultimately lead us home!

We are already powerful co-creators of realities. We simply have not been doing so from a conscious or "right-minded" perspective. The Mayan predictions about the end of cycles in 2012 simply stated that at this juncture we will all become "*conscious* co-creators of realities." We will awaken to the power we already have but have been blinded to by the same creative power that is misused in order to experience separation. On some level, I am pretty sure this is one of the reasons we are here on Earth—to become responsible and loving choice-makers who can be entrusted with greater creative possibilities in the future. How can we learn to manage worlds "out there" as hinted at by the *Star Trek* saying "To go where no man has gone before" until we get it together at home?

When you consciously exercise choice from an awakened state, you employ your mind as it was originally intended to be used, as an agent and extension of Creation. When you judge (think) out of conditioned fear, or retreat in guilt or shame, you are misusing your mind. You are exercising the power of your mind, but in the wrong direction. Your mind is going around in circles accomplishing nothing. No wonder so many intellectuals become depressed! No wonder academia has not truly helped to resolve many of our individual or global problems—academics are typically approaching problems with the "problem-making" mind, like a dog chasing its tail and getting nowhere while exhausting itself in the effort.

When you make a loving choice, one that is inclusive and forgiving, you are thinking like your Creator. You are becoming who you were before the spell of duality took place. Duality or "twoness" also implies movement. In duality mode, the mind never rests. It is always anticipating the next problem and planning how it will address this person, that situation—all from a frame of past references that often did not work either. How stressful is that?

It gets worse. When you consider the premise that perception itself is essentially divisive and illusory, and that all conflicts are simply the collision of illusions, it appears we spend a lot of time tied up in illusory knots of our own making. Eventually, we project this stress onto the body as sickness and depression.

When we choose to move past any specific dualistic conflict, however, there is a moment of neutrality, peace, and openness. We are simply more interested in recovering our peace in the moment than we are attached to one outcome or another. This is the first step toward sanity. Immediately, however, the verbal mind tries to capture this peace, give it a name, attribute a cause or attach it to a concept. But for a moment, no matter how fleeting, there was peace. It is like finding an oasis you didn't know was there. This is non-duality, and it is your natural state. The Course goes so far as to say, "Abstraction is the natural state of the mind." This implies that thinking and mental wrangling are not natural at all. Learning to quiet the mind through meditation is an invaluable skill for hastening the full return of your natural state. Becoming the awakened watcher of your thoughts puts you in a position to make clearer choices. I cannot emphasize enough the importance of learning to cultivate mental silence on a regular basis. The healing benefits for your mind and thus the body and the world are manifold.

Stillpoint

To illustrate the process of dissolving dualistic conflicts, consider the image above. On each side of the base of the pyramid we have the two sides of any potentially conflicting idea, belief, desire, quality, or perception. Any life area where we feel conflicted is game. Examples could be health versus illness, wealth versus poverty, happiness versus sadness, love versus fear, and so on. You can choose specifics or more general themes. One thing all these perceptions share, whether positive or negative, is that they all sustain conditional value judgments, or "taking a position" based on our preferences, biases, and conditioning. These are our "shoulds"—our inner demands on reality. Holding a position against opposition is quite stressful. While doing so may temporarily strengthen our ego-identity, it also increases our sense of inner division and thus creates anxiety. Our conflicts are always between illusions. We ask ourselves, "Which illusion do I want and which do I want to exclude?" Or perhaps more accurately, "Which illusion better supports my current illusion of self?"

There is no real peace or stillness in any set position we may take. The closer we get to one side of any issue, the stronger the pull of its opposite. Think of the bottom baseline of the pyramid as an elastic band. It is only when we tire of the strain that we realize that neither position leads to peace, and we are only hurting ourselves by our insistence. "Stress exists because *we* insist," goes the saying.

So we release attachment to either side of the story and find the exact midpoint on the line between the two opposites. The pull of either side perfectly balances at that one point, and we are instantly free of the "gravity" of the situation. We call this the *zero-point*. In zero-point, we are not only in zero gravity around a situation, but we also see clearly that there is zero-point in continuing the struggle!

Lifting off the line in neutral non-judgment, we naturally ascend to the third position, the top of the pyramid, where with the "all-seeing eye" of non-dual wisdom we can look at either side of the issue with complete non-attachment and then, if deemed appropriate, make choices from a place of win-win rather than win-lose. From the place above the battlefield our perspective is much broader. We can see possibilities we were blind to while we were toeing the line. The eye at the top is analogous to your 3D eye or Brow Chakra, the energy center that, when activated, reflects the Wisdom of the Master. This is the part of you that sees beyond the form of all they survey and laughs at the absurdity of perception, while understanding the field of perfection, the Spirit, which lies beyond the split mind. Here we access creativity rooted in Divine Love and the remembrance of Oneness.

Keep this image in mind the next time you are feeling conflicted. Ask Spirit to help you find that place of surrender and non-attachment at the middle point. Use your breath to focus your intent. By preferring peace in any situation, you are really seeking to experience something that is already yours. It is your birthright to know peace, harmony, health, and happiness all the time and in all situations. It is also your destiny.

Knowing that the world, others, and even our own self-concepts are all simply ideas held in the mind is liberating in and of itself. If everything is occurring in my mind, then I am always exactly where I need to be to make positive changes through good decisions. I have the power to change anything in my world by choosing to change my mind about it. I am a master, no longer a slave. If the world is in my mind and I am the choice-maker that sits above the mind, then I am a co-creator of realities now.

This understanding affirms that "All I ever experience is myself: my thoughts, my beliefs, my fears, my preferences, and the memory of my perfection underneath my illusions." I don't *really* experience you. I only experience myself experiencing you. If this is true for me, it is also true for you as you experience me. You don't really experience me; rather, you experience *yourself* experiencing an image of me held in your own mind. You experience your ideas, memories, judgments, desires, and mental associations and images that I represent to you. You can choose who I am to you, as I always choose who you are to me. That is how free we both are. That is how powerful we all are.

I encourage you again to find some kind of practice or technique that helps you to experience the neutral space within regularly, such as the Breath Meditation described earlier. This way you can learn to recognize the potential of your mind's inherent creativity, but also see that you have been neglecting or misusing this power by simply not recognizing your own conditioning, and you are now ready to take command and steer your mind in the direction of full recovery to wholeness. This will take a while, but there is no better use of time while we seem to be here in the dream of time, space, and bodies.

THE MIRROR WORLD

It is time to revisit the mirror analogy, perhaps with a deeper level of comprehension and appreciation. We can think of the world out there as a mirror, or, more accurately, a hall of mirrors. The world only gives back to us our state of mind in the moment. Our mental conditioning in reaction to the mirror-world is so instantaneous that we don't notice the tiny gap between primary, nonverbal perception and the mental imagery that immediately follows. The kind of revolutionary thinking we are proposing provides a correction for the misperception of the world as independently "real" and us as helpless victims of circumstances that appear to be outside of us and beyond our control.

A mirror is an interesting thing. When you walk into a small restaurant with a wall of mirrors, at first you may assume, "Wow, what a big place with lots of people! This must be a good restaurant!" Until, that is, you discover one wall is all mirrors, and all the people in the real restaurant are also in the "mirror" world, identical except they are all backward! This is why a mirror is such a great analogy for the nature of the world as we usually perceive it. Everything looks right on first glance, but on closer examination, it's all backward. In his novel *1984*, Orwell saw the world's institutions behaving as exact opposites of their self-proclaimed titles. We find eerie examples of this in today's mirror world.

"The Ministry of Truth" in Orwell's novel of the future cranked out a steady stream of propaganda. We have a "free press" that represents the views of a very small minority while remaining oblivious to any ideas that challenge the mainstream. Orwell's "Ministry of Peace" waged perpetual war. Sound close to home? It should, when you consider the actions of the current "Department of Defense," which has waged more than fifty economically motivated wars of devastation on innocent populations since the end of the Second World War. Consider the "World Health Organization" that stands behind dangerous unproven vaccines, the creation of AIDS as a bio-warfare weapon (see the work of Dr. Len Horowitz), and other public health catastrophes, the latest being the so-called 'Ebolagate' debacle. Why, for example, does the Centre for Disease control hold a patent on the Ebola virus? An alien observer could only conclude that this place is totally insane!

With this mirror-model in mind, you can take any entrenched dogma or belief system in the world today and safely assume that the opposite must be true! However, many are caught in the mirror world, identified with their self-image rather than the true Self, and simply do not see the incongruence of the images they live among. This is because, on some level, we *wanted* the mirror world as a place to hide in. To hide from what?

Our guilt-laden ego has created a false fear of the truth of our being: that we remain Divine, innocent, invulnerable, and eternal Spiritual beings having a human experience. Why did we want to hide from such a liberating truth? The problem is and was the guilt we feel for a crime we did not commit, but believed we did. We are like a prisoner with a life sentence who realizes that the door is only locked from the inside, and he had the key all along.

Realizing that the mirror world, in which we placed so much trust, is nothing but a lie can be a severe shock to our minds. This is why some people who experiment with mind-expanding drugs or plant medicines without adequate preparation and understanding can be thrown into a psychological tailspin. The shattering of our false worldview is one of the risks of the dissolving of the ego. We can accomplish the same liberation from illusions much more gently by allowing ideas like the kind we are discussing to gradually introduce us and open our minds bit by bit to a more expanded sense of Self, until we fully recover from our dream of separation, awake and ready to joyfully face a new day.

In terms of relationship, we can now begin to appreciate that each interaction we experience mirrors the state of our own minds in the moment, albeit the meaning we give the interaction may be the opposite of the truth. Knowing this, we can pause and make a conscious decision to see the "real person" behind the behavior or words, and in so doing we may expect to see our "real self" reflecting back to us. If we are convinced of our own innocence and worthiness and are committed to the healing of the unconscious guilt in our minds, then we may find ourselves automatically extending the gift of non-judgment in the form of mental silence over meaningless ego content in our interactions. Relationships, having been re-purposed, become the source of continual self-discovery and recovery of the reality of love.

THIRTEEN

Perspective: Creation Story Part 2

We need to step back and gain the broadest perspective possible so we can confidently re-enter the mirror world and begin to set things right. Not for everybody else, but for ourselves. How can we presume to be of any assistance to the sleepwalkers caught in the mirror world until we awaken ourselves? This is job number one. When this is achieved, all the rest will fall into place naturally. You will know what to do. You will know how to forgive.

In order to reinforce the basis for our awakening, we will look again, perhaps with more depth, at how we got where we are and why forgiveness holds the promise to undo it all.

You certainly don't need to agree with the story I am about to tell. It is a story, however, that has shown up in one form or another since the dawn of history, a story referred to by author Aldous Huxley as the "Perennial

Philosophy." These are the great truths that have somehow stayed in mankind's awareness in one form or another over eons, and are at the root of all religions in their truest and purest forms. I have found in my spiritual coaching work that grasping the origins of our common situation and the "one problem" at the root of all problems helps to lessen the belief in the false premise of separation we all assume to be real. Knowing we are living out a collective agreement takes the sting out of our suffering and challenges the assumption that we are all alone in our individual stories. The personal stories may be unique in form, but they all are variations on one theme. What follows is a review and amplification of the story as related in an earlier section.

Are we all comfy? Then let us begin.

Before time, space, or anything in existence, there was Creator (who doesn't mind what name we use to describe him/her/it). It really is impossible to describe this Being in words, and many words have been attempted and twisted and countless lives destroyed over the disagreement of descriptions of this Being. So let's suffice to say that this Supreme Being or Prime Creator has always existed as the cause of All That Is. This Being is beyond form and in a complete and harmonious state within Itself.

Because this Being knows nothing of conflict, opposition, or separation within itself, you could say that "all things are possible" within it. This includes all possible thoughts or ideas, including something as crazy as the idea of separation. Perhaps the idea arose in a form such as "Gee, this is great, but what would it be like to have an experience outside of All There Is?" or, more succinctly, "What if I could do this (exist) all by myself?" In our insistence, we were like the little child who impulsively grabs the steering wheel because they don't know any better, thinking they can drive just like a grownup.

This was the first thought of separation. Allowing all things and resisting nothing, Creator lovingly tolerated the wish. Creator likely knew where the idea would lead, but was willing to let us "play." It knew the idea had come from some aspect of itself, so could not really resist or deny the idea from its holy (whole) state of perfection.

The release of the idea of separation provided the impetus behind the Big Bang. The idea was the formless cause; the Universe became the effect of the idea on the level of form or matter. From of the state of perfect, changeless Oneness came a Universe of "split" or separate forms that started off at the subatomic level. Particles were generated in pairs. (Modern physicists now agree that every subatomic particle exists in complete unity with its double, no matter how far they may be separated in space.) This was the beginning of duality emerging from the original non-dual state of pure Being.

The Big Bang was the answer to *our request* to experience something other than perfect union. You might wonder, "Why would a loving Creator allow this to happen, knowing full well how the desire for and consequent belief in separation would be the cause of such overwhelming suffering for humanity and all of nature? Who would allow such a cruel thing?" This is where we become tempted to blame God for what *we* did, like the juvenile delinquent who blames his behavior on his "bad parents." "If Dad didn't hide the car keys, I wouldn't have found them!"

Here's the clincher, and the part that, when you "get it," is the crack in the armor of the illusion we call "me, the world, and the Universe." The mirror world begins to dissolve, revealing the brilliance of the light of truth it once obscured.

This is the question we must consider: "If God or the Creator represents All That Is or Oneness, could this Oneness actually be divided in reality, and *still remain One?*" Put another way, is separation from Oneness possible at all if Oneness remains as One? And if separation is not possible, what the heck is the Universe, and who the hell am I? This is the question we have been trying to answer for eons. The best we could come up with in our amnesia was the ego, a fabricated set of images and ideas about who we *think* we are.

In case you're wondering, I will tell you straight. Separation from Oneness is *not possible* if Oneness is to remain as one. "Twoness" would negate Oneness. So if "twoness" or separation from Oneness is not possible, what you are left with is an impossibility, right? What is a good analogy for an impossible event that *appears* to exist or be possible? The best example I know of is an illusion, or perhaps better, a dream.

In a dream, no matter how bizarre the events get, or "out of this world" you feel you are, have you left your body? Have you left the comfort of your bed? Of course not. But you don't know this in the dream state, because in that state, the dream *is* your reality. All your attention and sense of self appears to be completely absorbed by the dream. It is only upon awakening that you realize you were only dreaming, and you can ignore everything you thought happened, whether you judged it good or bad at the time.

With this in mind, let's back up and review the story. Within Oneness was a desire to experience separation. Knowing this was not possible, yet honoring the Being that wanted it (*us* as the true and original Creation), Creator arranged for the idea to birth a dream—a vision if you like—of what separation would be like. Now this idea was actually birthed in the mind of the one Prime Creation, and quickly took on a reality of its own with all of the power we as the One True Creation have. The idea itself was a bona fide "Creation" within Creator, but what we "created" was only an impossible dream. More accurately, the Universe is our mis-creation. To put the pieces together, consider this syntax: Prime Creator (existing always) births us, the Prime Creation, which births the Universe out of a desire to experience itself as separate. The prodigal Son leaves home for a life of adventure, or so it thinks.

What we have been discussing here is no less than a complete denial and negation of practically every belief of every dreamer who has ever dreamed here. Yet what is it that we truly "know"? What we call "truth" is more often a set of beliefs that have been handed down to us by generations of fellow dreamers, often instilled in us before the skills of critical thinking are developed. Even after we start to think for ourselves, the pressure of the herd mentality around us often prevents us from peeking outside the consensus reality we assume is All There Is. If you choose to look outside the dream, you may find yourself crucified, or diagnosed, which often become the same thing. If the foundation of the world is an insane premise, are the "insane" the ones who found this out and couldn't fake it any longer? Or are we simply "going sane" as we awaken to the grand deception of this world?

The true Creation story, as outlined here and in the Course, answers a big question many people ask when they ponder the pointless pain and stressful struggle of the world: "How could God create such an insane and painful world?" Simple: He didn't. We did! The "God" of dualistic religion, being partially loving and partially wrathful, is more accurately a projected self-image of a schizophrenic human mental state that is split between our Divine and self-made (ego) identities. Consistent with the false mirror world, the God of human dualistic religions is clearly "made in our image."

If this world of striving until you drop is in truth merely a convincing dream-illusion, would it not make sense to do all we can to bring the dream to its conclusion and awaken back to Ourselves and get on with life? Of course it would. And we have been given the tools and support we need once we are willing to recognize them.

Many of these tools have been handed down by those who have achieved awakening or mastery in the past. Not only have these teachers left us with words of wisdom and practices that truly heal, but they have also established in the collective mind a template and precedent for everyone to eventually access that knowledge and call it their own.

How is this possible? Although on the level of the body, we seem to be separate dreamers experiencing our own unique time-space events, on the level of the mind, we are still as we started out—One. Bodies are physical and thus subject to the Newtonian laws of physicality. Mind is non-physical, and subject to quantum realities. Mind is thus unlimited by time or space (non-local), powerful in its creative potential (observer effect), and unlimited in its potential (indeterminacy). We get into trouble when we try to apply the laws of one dimension to dimensions where those laws do not operate. The ego-mind will use these apparent contradictions as justification for its own doubts and disbelief, often masking its cynicism as "healthy skepticism." A skeptic doubts, but is open to evidence that can prove a position. A cynic has made up his mind and does not want to be confused by evidence contrary to his beliefs.

Let's see how the practice of True Forgiveness may be the fastest way to wake up from the illusion of separation. Be forewarned, though; once you start to awaken, there really is no going back. It is like that first glimpse of daylight coming through the shades in the morning. You know that waking up is now inevitable, waiting only on your willingness to throw off the fog of dreams and covers of illusion and face the new day.

By awakening, I don't mean dying and leaving the current dream you are having. Just as it is possible to awaken within the dream state as in episodes of lucid dreaming, so it is possible to awaken spiritually in this world and still appear to walk around in the dream. The difference is that once you wake up in the dream and start living lucidly, you begin to live with fearless invulnerability. You know nothing is as it appears, and that you, as the dreamer of the dream, are safe at home—the home you never left. The values of the dream world that used to drag you down or pull you into distraction, causing pain through endless striving and feelings of lack and failure, are now meaningless to you. You know you are absolutely free to walk out of the theatre any time you wish. Yet being here in the dream does offer some unique opportunities for the awakening dreamer. Namely, you can reach out to other dreamers who slumber, still disguised as another figure in your dream, and gently nudge them awake. You can speed the awakening of the One Dreamer, one seemingly separate dreamer at a time. We do this by putting attention on our relationships—the richest resource we have for extending the healing balm of forgiveness.

FOURTEEN

The Problem of Guilt

We typically experience guilt over something we have done or think we have done in the past. In a way, this kind of guilt can help guide us to make better choices, make amends, and change for the better—*if* we listen to the guilt, take it as instruction, and then forgive. Unfortunately, our "outer guilt" for things we think we have done activates a much deeper unconscious guilt of which we are typically not aware.

But what if this deep, unconscious guilt was for something you *didn't* do? What if it was based on the erroneous assumption that the separation you desired before the Creation of the Universe actually happened? What if this unfounded guilt had the ability to seriously disrupt your healthy functioning, even in your dream world, as appeared in Dr. Hamer's discoveries? Wouldn't this be a tragedy of epic proportions? And what if this deep, unfounded guilt was part of everyone's experience on planet Earth from time immemorial, and was responsible for *all* of the suffering we have experienced here? After all, our hate, prejudice, and anger is nothing other than a projection of our own guilt onto a seeming "other" in an attempt to get rid of it. Would it not be reasonable to investigate this guilt and see if there is a way to remove it? Do you think the outcome of erasing guilt would be worth the effort? Only you can answer that question for yourself.

Going back to our metaphysical premise for a moment, the first effect of our mutual decision to experience separation (which created time, space, and bodies) was the dreadful suspicion that we actually pulled it off . . . but in doing so, we must have destroyed if not seriously offended Oneness, God, our Creator. Somehow we tore ourselves from the perfect fabric of the original Creation in a selfish whim to have "more than everything." Oh, the guilt that followed! That sense of isolation and separation was so painful and full of regret that we could not bear the possibility that we had done this. We learned to stuff our guilt deep in the unconscious mind, where it would then re-emerge as projection.

An immediate assumption, in our own need to defend our separation, was that perhaps we didn't abandon Creator; rather, Creator abandoned us! Clearly, Creator must not love us to just let us wander off. Think of the terror a small child feels when they discover their mother is no longer holding their hand and they are lost in a huge crowd. Multiply that a few billion times to get an idea of the abject terror we felt. This was the ultimate nightmare, while all along we were "safe at home while dreaming of exile."

All of our human hurts and dramas are really a reliving of this original pain. The pains of this life are minimal next to the ontological pain of the belief in separation from our Source. The terror of a lost child is a dream-echo of our collective terror in being born into a Universe of separation. We have been living out a schizophrenic nightmare ever since. In order to accept the belief that separation actually happened, we had to deny and reject the knowledge of Oneness. I have referred to this deep guilt as *unfounded* because the *guilt is not based in reality*. It is therefore based in illusion, much as any event in a dream. You may still be asking, however, "Why did the 'Oneness' agree to this travesty of reality?"

Oneness is another name for unconditional love. As part of Oneness, there is nothing we could do that could change the fact that the love that created us is irrevocable and not dependent on any condition or affected by change of any kind, real or imagined. Our desire to experience separation, no matter how whimsical it may have been, occurred within a perfect "circle of trust." Creator could not deny the Creation's choice, for to do so would have been an act of fear—the need to "protect" us from something outside of ourselves. Oneness cannot and does not conceive of anything outside itself, as there is nothing there. There was nothing real to protect us from.

Think of a loving father taking his daughter to the park to play. When the child sees the playground and other children, she runs off to play, feeling exuberant and falsely independent in order to exercise her imagination and create all kinds of fun fantasies. As the child builds castles in the sandbox, the parent sits on the bench and watches, knowing full well that his daughter's mind is far away and totally wrapped up in fantasies and images.

The father knows that no harm can come to this child, even if she should pretend in her playtime to be slain by dragons or swallowed up in storms. These things are only "happening" in her mind. The father recognizes his own creative nature in his daughter, and smiles at her potential to create worlds of wonder and discovery. He watches lovingly, knowing that this phase in his daughter's development is necessary for her to discover on her own her power to create. The child is in a learning phase, which cannot be rushed. She must be allowed to do what she wishes within the freedom, confidence, and trust that "knowing all" brings.

Eventually the child tires of playing. As children mature, they begin to move into more responsible modes of behavior. The father, seeing himself in the child, knows she is an equal and a "co-creator" in training, learning to create from love and, eventually and inevitably, the desire for a complete return to Oneness. This desire was placed there as part of the child's inheritance, and it must come to fruition eventually. Nothing in or beyond the Universe can stop or prevent this from happening. The dreamer must awaken.

We are at a critical awakening point on the planet. The current epidemic of depression and mental/emotional issues, especially in the so-called "developed" world, is symptomatic of this wave of change, despite appearances. In the modern world, we do not yet have a place in the social milieu for the new shamans and wise ones awakening in our midst. The day for us to recognize the true teachers among us is dawning, as it must. The way that we learn from each other must shift from a top-down transfer of controlled information to a horizontal appreciation of the truth and beauty hidden within our everyday experiences and interactions. Thus, we will become both learners and teachers with every encounter in a continuous expansive process of discovery and joy.

Even though the guilt borne of the belief in separation is totally unfounded, once we set our course upon awakening, everything, including this "guilt for having been born," turns to serve that purpose. The guilt then becomes the source of what we call "Divine discontent"—the feeling that "something here is 'off' and I'm going to do something about it!" If you are reading this now, on some level, you must have made the same determination. Otherwise you would not have been attracted to this information. You are ready! *Now* is the time to begin to shake off the false layers of guilt in your mind. Forgive your projections and allow the Immortal Light Being that you are to emerge.

REMOVING GUILT

Given that guilt has been with us since the beginning, removing guilt can seem like a daunting task, if not an impossibility. In this suffering world, the more you look the more you see the results of our belief in our separation in the form of endless wars, poverty, disease, inequality, and the resultant effort to "fix" these things on the level of effect rather than cause. Guilt-based efforts will never address or effectively remove guilt. One of the ego's favorite cul-de-sacs is called "good intentions." We have discovered in our healing work that we often work through issues over many (seemingly separate) lifetimes, playing out roles of either victim, perpetrator, or rescuer around a certain theme or life issue like a game of cosmic musical chairs. The "rescuer" role is the toughest one to appreciate as an integral part of the illusion, as it is always so well-intended. Yet in putting attention on solving problems on the level of effect only, the rescuer is inadvertently making the problem real, and thus ensuring that the cycles of guilt, pain, and suffering continue. Isn't it interesting that in chemistry, to "fix" a compound is to make it stable, consistent, and resistant to change? Is this what we want to do with our problems and for those we purport to care about? In the noble but misguided attempt to help someone get out of the problem, we often end up helping them dig a deeper hole. The key to dissolving guilt is realizing its unreality and correcting the level of cause in the mind. Until then, only the form of suffering changes; the content remains the same.

Once we truly begin to see the deep dysfunction operating in this world, we can become quite discouraged at the prospect of turning the world around. Be assured, however, that you are not being asked to do the impossible, only to embrace what is possible and what, in a sense, has already been accomplished on your behalf. You are not responsible for anyone's awakening other than your own. Set your relationships free from the projections of your mind, and set yourself free in the process. It is absolutely true that you are only experiencing yourself, and this is true for everyone in your world. Thinking we have to "change the world" before we can have peace or sanity ourselves is typical "mirror world" logic. Turn the assumption around, and you find all you need do is change your mind about the world—what it means to you and what opportunities are presented to you in your everyday experiences. You have stepped into your power to not only change yourself, but ultimately your world, which does begin to change in the direction you wanted all along! Not because you forced change on anyone else—you were simply smart and courageous enough to accept that "the world is as I am." You shifted from "flipping out" to "flipping in."

Guilt has many faces. Overt suffering, illness, and conflict are the obvious ones. Guilt can also motivate the healer, the "do-gooder," and the one who takes on the mantle of "fixing the problem out there" rather than turning to the cause of the problem within, as noted above. It is with noble intention that we spend lifetimes trying to change the image on the screen while neglecting the projector in our minds. It is really just a matter of misplaced intention. As the aphorism goes, "The road to hell is paved with good intentions." We are so fixated on the forms of illusion (bodies, nature, the world, the Universe) that we lose sight of the cause of these things in our own minds.

One way we keep ourselves distracted is in the dance of the mutually supportive false identities we take on over many lifetimes. As far as reincarnation goes, it only makes sense that life continues beyond the demise of the body. The Law of Conservation of Energy dictates that energy (in this case, life itself) cannot be destroyed; it can only change from one form to another. We like to think of our "past lives" as somehow personal and special to us alone. This is understandable; we like to think we are separate and "special" people. From the perspective of Oneness, though, there is and has only ever been One of us here. There are no "others," just you in your various disguises and costumes. So you, as an extension of the One Mind, the Christ, are in fact living all lives at once. That concept is too big for most rational minds to entertain. That's okay. Now that you've heard it, there's no going back, and you will "get it"—this is the truth about you and all of us! There may be, however, specific lifetime memories that are more instructive to your chosen pathway of awakening. We call these "our" past or future lives, or more accurately and from a quantum perspective, parallel lives all happening at once.

We forget there's really only one problem here—all the rest are echoes of that one problem, which is our belief in separation. The well-meaning but misguided "rescuer" is what the Course refers to as a "wounded healer"; that is, someone who is compelled to help everyone else with their problems so they don't have to face the one problem within themselves. The ego fully supports the wounded healer, as the wounded healer's self-image is of a concerned and loving helper. The wounded healer does not see the damage done by making problems real; how essentially disempowering it is to those who have masterfully created their "problems" in order to awaken. I am not suggesting that we be unkind or inconsiderate. It is one thing to be naturally helpful and concerned for the welfare and comfort of others; it is simply a higher path to know when to release others from our judgment of them as anything less than powerful and capable. If we see the "master" behind the situation, there is a much greater possibility that those we love and care for will realize this master within themselves more readily. We can decide to release them to the freedom to experience the effects of their own choices.

"Please don't 'fix' my problems! I need them to help me awaken. If you 'fix' me too soon, I may need to come back lifetime after lifetime to recognize the real problem and heal. I must do this on my own as I am free to choose to awaken and will do so only when I am truly ready."

The solution to the "one problem" again is the only solution that will work. And that is in recognizing and accepting Spirit's gift of the correction of our minds, and the opportunity to return to our own wholeness through releasing ourselves from our wounded and split mind. This is best done through giving and receiving forgiveness.

The good news, again, is that it is not your responsibility to fix the whole mess. The Course emphatically states, "We do not try to fix the world. Rather we choose to see the world differently." The solution to our belief in separation was actually given the split second it occurred. The Course calls this solution the *atonement* or simply the *correction*. Our job as (seeming) individuals is to recognize and accept the correction already given *for ourselves*. This correction exists as an idea, much as we do. The idea is this: "The separation never happened in reality, and therefore there is no basis for your guilt, anger, or pain. Nothing in reality was changed by your decision to fall asleep and dream of separation. Accept this now, and you are free. And . . . oh yes . . . I have always loved you."

All you are called to do is awaken from your personal dream of separation. Everything else will fall into place when this becomes your prime focus. You are "programmed" in a sense for this to occur, like an egg is programmed to become a chicken. It is never a question of "Will I ever awaken?" It is only a question of when. And that, my friend, is entirely up to you . . . to accept, not accomplish. Your Creator has absolute trust in you to awaken at the perfect time. From the perspective of eternity, it has already happened. You can truthfully and honestly tell yourself "I am fully awakened," and in doing so you are affirming what has always been real and true about you outside the illusion of time.

We are confronted here with the paradox of free will. Is it truly free? Well, yes and no. In the context of your eternal and immortal soul, you have no choice. You are what you are, as you are created. Nothing changes that, ever. Within the context of the story we call life, yes, you can determine outcomes by the choices you make—again, within the unchanging reality of your True Self. So free will is more like the kind of free will a parent offers a child: "You can mow the lawn, babysit your sister, or do your homework. You are absolutely free to choose!" I suppose the deeper benefit of this conditional free will is that we ultimately do get to choose the moment of awakening, when we discover that our free will was and is always one with the Divine Will. This is the setup for the perfect cosmic joke! Everything was in the script all along, and we wrote it!

Once we accept these premises and start to claim the freedom that is our birthright, we begin to see the path of our lives heading in a new direction. Yet a path through time still seemingly remains. This is another paradox: "I am beginning to see I am a Divine, Immortal, and Innocent being, so why am I still here in this nuthouse world and failing body?" You are here to *fully* awaken. So far, you have had "awakening moments" that will eventually merge into a "steady state" of being fully awakened. But if full awakening happened all at once, you as a human projection may not be able to handle the influx of light and energy coming through, and you certainly wouldn't be much good to fellow dreamers who are still caught in the nets of illusion. In fact, the Course tells us we will never truly return to full Divine knowledge while here in a body. But we can certainly head in that direction, knowing where we are headed and having a good time while we do.

You are here primarily to clean out every little dark corner of your mind where unconscious guilt lingers, and your relationships offer you this opportunity, especially if they do not yet all reflect 100 percent peace and harmony. If you were 100 percent awakened here and now, you would have mastered guilt and moved on to another realm of operation, or you would be here as a *bodhisattva* or Ascended Master returned to Earth School in service to the One. But the fact that you *are* still here in a body having a human experience means you still have work to do. Your name is on the graduation list, but there are a few final classes to take. And this work is showing up in the relationships that offer you an opportunity to forgive. To be clear, it is not *really* others that you forgive; it is the unconscious guilt you have projected onto those who you are forgiving each time that you actually forgive as you put judgment aside in favor of healing.

In other words, and to repeat and reinforce a very important idea, the most effective and efficient way to remove all remaining vestiges of guilt is to deal with your own projections of guilt in the form of relationships. Relationships will faithfully reflect back to you the state of your mind in the moment. Each relationship that disturbs your peace is offering you a mirror of some part of your mind that you have withheld so far from the "correction" already given. By being willing to forgive the relationship in front of you, you demonstrate that you are willing to give up the guilt in your own mind that the relationship brought to light. In this way, *all* relationships serve you and your awakening, just as you serve these relationships by your example of forgiveness. Your life now has a new purpose, and the results are guaranteed!

Many people wonder what their life's purpose is. They wonder if their feelings of unhappiness may be tied to simply not doing what they are here to do. We often think this "life purpose" will appear in some grand flash of insight, with a new opportunity to take our lives on a new and exotic journey. Not to say this can't happen, but what if it doesn't?

When Eckhart Tolle was asked about life purpose, his typically elegant and straightforward reply was that everyone's life purpose is the same: to awaken. Your immediate life's purpose lies in whatever you are doing in the moment toward that end. So the purpose of our life is not measured in the outward form of what we do, but simply in *the purpose we give to whatever we are doing!*

Giving yourself the purpose of awakening through the practice of true forgiveness is the highest calling to which anyone can aspire, and it provides the fastest pathway to the fulfillment of your own joy, freedom, and liberation. Given the gift that forgiveness offers you, is there any good reason not to choose this path?

FIFTEEN

The Healing Power of Forgiveness

Hopefully by now we have laid the foundation for an understanding and appreciation of the "setup" here in our dream of life on Earth. As mentioned earlier, I prefer to think of this planet as Earth School as a reminder of the most useful way to think about our experiences and purpose here. If we are not here to learn, what, really, is the point of being here at all? Everything the world has to offer eventually fades back into the nothingness and "dream stuff" it came from. The glitter of worldly achievements quickly becomes dull in the light of day. And the ego always wants more and more of this nothingness.

The ego is heavily invested in time, and thus the belief that it must prevent the "terrible past" from recurring in the "fearful future" no matter how well things are actually going in the present. No wonder suicide is rampant. When folks realize the pointlessness of the separated existence and have not yet tapped into their truth, their lives can be very discouraging indeed. This irrational fear is mitigated by the fact that we cannot die. The suicidal, after arriving in the Spirit world too soon and without a reservation, are simply given another ticket back to Earth School to pick up where they left off in their learning, with the need to go through the arduous growing up process all over again. The "cosmic plan" has all of us winning eventually. We choose the duration of the journey and the degree of apparent suffering we need in order to wake us up.

In the breakthrough work *Destiny of Souls*, Dr. Michael Newton documented how the experience of the lucid dream is similar to the experience of the out-of-body state we call a near-death experience (NDE). (Come to think of it, we are all just one breath away from our own NDE.) While under deep hypnosis, many of Newton's patients recalled their "between lives" experiences and remembered meeting with their guides in the Spirit world. In these meetings with Spirit, the patients planned the course of the next incarnation after a full life review and perhaps some remedial guidance.[17] Apparently, we plan every minute detail of our next incarnation; who our parents and siblings will be, what jobs we will have, even what period of history we will live in, all to give us the very best opportunities to awaken to our Divine Nature within a human incarnation.

It is only because we pass through the "veil of forgetting" at birth that we think we can be victim to anything

....

17. Michael Newton, *Destiny of Souls* (St. Paul, MN: Llewellyn, 2004).

not of our own choosing. If we really understood that *we* planned every circumstance, relationship, and challenge in our lives from the very beginning, we would have no basis for blaming anyone for anything. With the realization of our life plan as the best and most beneficial plan we could imagine, we can relax into acceptance that, despite appearances, whatever "Is" is for our highest good. "Responsibility" means the ability to respond with understanding rather than reacting from the conditioned ego, the sleeping mind. As true understanding without forgiving is impossible, the ultimate responsibility to ourselves is to offer and thus receive forgiveness.

I want to tie together some ideas now. When we truly grasp what is going on when we are in conflict or judgment in a relationship, we have more choices at our disposal. If I believe that every attack on me is coming from some outside threat alone, I am forever cast in the role of victim, either actual or potential. This limited perspective condemns one to a life sentence of living under the tyranny of fear. Here we see the ego's purpose fulfilled: It keeps us limited to a separated, suffering concept of the self for its own survival's sake. As a self-perpetuating set of beliefs, the ego is highly invested in its own survival. The fact that it correctly suspects you will inevitably discover it has no reality only drives it deeper into itself and strengthens its conviction to survive at all costs . . . even at the cost of your physical life. As usual, even if it should 'succeed' in it's madness, the joke is on the ego, as there is no death, only a transition of energy from one form to another. The fear of physical death is one of the last aces up the ego's sleeve. The ego has convinced us to fear only a mirage—another illusion with no basis in truth or reality.

A fundamental concept in our growth toward spiritual maturity and empowerment has been offered already—namely, the idea that *"All I ever experience is myself."* As long as I am blaming something or someone outside of myself for my poor, unfortunate circumstances, I deny the power invested in me by virtue of my Divine Creator. We call self-denial "humility," but in fact it is egoic pride. By thinking "I am not worthy," I am in effect saying to my Creator, "My low opinion of myself is more credible than your high opinion of me."

The next time you are in conversation with someone, try this exercise. Mentally "step back" from the conversation and observe yourself from a silent place. See how you are actually more engaged with *your* thoughts about the person—what to say next, how to "read" them, and so on—than you are interested in truly connecting with them behind their words and body. Are you really experiencing them, or are you reacting to a past image of this person you already hold in your mind? This is a subtle but crucial distinction. Realize that in every exchange, you are operating on at least two levels at once. The level of the ego-mind is the one that is planning, calculating, looking for advantage, and trying to second guess the other's motivations while maintaining a pleasant exterior. Alternatively, the ego is condescendingly dismissive of what it hears in its penchant for comparing and categorizing. It has already judged the speaker based on its own past experience and internal mental image of them. The ego then becomes impatient, angry, or belligerent as it judges the person unworthy of its precious time and attention. No matter how "nice" the exterior we present, the ego is only ever afraid for its own survival.

You are in that same moment communing as Spirit to Spirit, as One Self to ItSelf. On this level you recognize the Light of your True Self looking back at you through the eyes of the other. The differences between you become inconsequential as your Spirits dance in mutual recognition and celebration. This was the meaning behind the salutation the characters in the movie Avatar used to greet each other: "I see you!" and in the Mayan greeting "In Lak'ech Ala K'in," which means "I am another yourself." Again, knowing you are always operating on at least two levels at once can empower you with the option to choose which modality you want to identify with and operate from—the real Self or the pseudo, made-up self. You will be able to reflect and determine which Self you were relating from, based solely on the feelings you have after an interaction. Once you decide to operate from your real Self, you may find a lot of opposition from the false selves you were relating to previously. This is when many people find out who their real friends are. Don't worry if you lose a few "friends" in the process of awakening. Your example will never leave them, and you will find new acquaintances who will mirror your new decision for peace over pain.

We are seeing this happen more and more lately. When you walk down the street your eyes might "lock" with another set of eyes momentarily in a flash of recognition. This happens for a split second before the "logical" (ego) mind steps in and tells you "You've never met this person before . . . how could there be recognition of someone you don't even know?"

On the level of Spirit or reality, we *do* know everyone. This is because we are already One with every person who has ever or will ever be born onto this planet, even in this Universe. There is only One of us here, remember? Right now, this may seem like a far-out New Age idea. If, however, you allow this idea to consistently inform you and begin to choose this level of perception regularly, the idea will inevitably become your reality. The thought will become a feeling and then a knowing. But the experiential knowing starts with entertaining the thought. This is why study, repetition, and the application of key ideas until they fully integrate is a necessary step in our awakening, at this stage of the game at least.

You may be asking yourself, "How might I be able to do this, to maintain the knowledge of Oneness, when for the most part I am caught up in the experience of the moment, and much more likely to react as I am conditioned to than to pause and reconsider the options in the heat of the event?" Asking this question is evidence of growing self-awareness.

The answer to this very important question is in embracing the power you have to choose to forgive rather than judge. Never fear—this can be done just as effectively with past relationships as with those in your present life—even years later after, once we calm down and recognize our own reactive patterns. Remember the mind is non-local, and so can just as easily affect the past as the present or future. Recall our discussion of how linear time is illusion; in fact, all events are happening at once in an expanded field of "now."

When I choose to forgive you, who am I really choosing to forgive, anyway? I am really choosing to forgive my perception of you and thus change myself. I am choosing to see you through my own innocent eyes (my Spiritual sight) rather than the ego eye's seeing through the filter of guilt and separation. It really is that simple. We realize we *do* have a choice in what we experience, and then we make that choice. When I extend forgiveness for what I perceive to be a lack or fault or "sin" in you, I am in truth discovering a part of my mind where I still hold a little dark patch of my own guilt. After all, my image of you is a projection of my own mind, and nothing else. When I allow for a new experience of you, I am instructing my own mind to release that guilt, and the Divine Light of love which is the motivation behind the decision for peace over conflict fills the space in my mind, and I become "enlightened" (or at least one big step closer).

As for letting go of judgment, many people judge themselves harshly for not being able to do so consistently. To judge ourselves for being judgmental is like the dog chasing its tail—eternally frustrating! The real freedom from judgment comes from a couple of realizations. One is that *all thought is judgment.* You can't get away from this fact. A thought separates something we have chosen to elevate in importance above all else from All That Is, and so we automatically judge the thought as worthy and all else as unrelated and thus unworthy of attention. In other words, thoughts divide. Any form of division carries with it the subtle memory of our own belief in separation, and the fear and guilt that followed.

Couple this with the idea that my thoughts are essentially meaningless. They carry only the meaning I choose to give them out of past reference, but of themselves, they represent nothing. Therefore, I'm not *really* judging with my thoughts. I only think I am.

The real freedom from judgment comes from the liberating realization that *"I cannot judge."* Therefore I can automatically forgive my own thoughts, even as they spew forth, knowing I am not doing anything real at all. If judgment is as meaningless as my thoughts, what's the point? So the idea here is not that "I *shouldn't* judge!" (. . . as that's a judgment—all "shoulds" are subtle demands) but rather "I cannot judge, and therefore release myself and you of the unnecessary and laughable 'benefit' of my judgments."

An important transition from the strictly personal to the impersonal begins to dawn on the mind devoted to healing. As we are already One, my "personal" healing, in truth, benefits everyone. There comes a point in the healing journey when we start to see patterns in our process, showing up as the same issues reappearing in slightly different forms. For some, this can be a source of frustration when we feel we should be done with a particular issue. I have heard from many personal clients over time, "I thought I was done with that issue!" Consider, though, that after you successfully release that thing within yourself, you are qualified to extend that healing out to others who, after all, are One with you. In fact, if someone else out there is still suffering from the same thing, can you honestly say you have completely healed that thing for yourself? It all depends on which "self" you are referring to: the ego who thinks you are your isolated and vulnerable body, or your immortal, Innocent Self who is One with all. As you ponder this possibility, your orientation shifts from "service to self" to "service to others." Once they are "de-personalized," problems lose their ability to keep us limited or afraid. They are simply our chosen path through Earth School and are part of our service for the highest good.

We may still do the same things on our personal healing journey, but with a broader, more inclusive purpose. This brings the natural fruits of joy, as anything we do that joins us together with others is in alignment with love's purpose, which is union over separation. We discover that "service to self" is rather pointless, as there is no real separate self to begin with! All of our healing efforts have always been in service to the One all along! Another cosmic joke!

For most of us the process of "stumbling toward the Light" has taken many lifetimes. We are now at a critical juncture and opportunity in the "plan" where we may be moving into the Light en masse. Ken Carey has observed that the last two thousand years was a period of Individual Awakening, where through hard work and devotion, it was possible for some—very few actually—to fully awaken spiritually. We are now at the threshold of a thousand-year period of Planetary Awakening where enlightenment may become the new normal. Can you imagine a whole planet of Ascended Masters? If you can, you are helping to manifest it now.

Understanding the level of truth we have been discussing enables us to be keenly aware of the modality we are choosing in each moment—Spirit or ego? Love or fear?—and to make a new choice. There is no pressure from any person or Being outside of you to do this. We gain motivation when we see the difference that choosing peace brings to our lives and relationships. It is said that no one knowingly hurts themselves. If we are hurting ourselves through projection, blame, and acting as victims, it is because we are not acting out of knowledge, we are acting from past conditioning and false belief, or ego.

Thus, the best gift we can offer is to focus on our own "wholeness" or healing. By putting the healing of my own mind above my concern for fixing others or the world on the level of form or effect, I am stepping into the level of causation and service to others beyond anything my good intentions could possibly imagine or achieve anyway.

I can be confident that because I am now operating at the level of cause rather than effect, the healing I experience and extend through forgiveness will be true, effective, and ever-lasting.

SIXTEEN

The Resolve to Awaken

I must decide to see each relationship I encounter as first a relationship with my Self. I can then own my own will and power of choice, and can act from true intelligence. I begin to see you, no matter what your behavior may appear to be on the surface, as my perfect teacher, even as a savior from my own illusions. I have drawn you into my script so that you can mirror to me the part of my mind that is still in need of healing, that still holds a vestige of the past. The One Self we both represent has conspired perfectly to create an opportunity for its own healing and recovery through this relationship, should I choose to take the opportunity.

Imagine if enough people on Earth did this all at once. Would we drop all the ridiculous fears and prejudices that have only served the ego and its thirst for conflict? Would we be the fulfillment of the motto from the 1960s peace movement, "What if they gave a war and nobody came?"

I must determine within myself to remain vigilant with my own thoughts before attempting to "read" meaning into others' thoughts. I need to recognize the voice of the ego (critical, jumping to conclusions, judging, separating, comparing, and complaining) versus the Voice of Spirit (quiet, neutral, accepting, non-reactive, inclusive, and loving) and then make a choice.

The ego is usually the first to speak up—often loudly and belligerently. The ego typically makes broad claims such as "He's such a loser" or "Women are all like that." It will then pat you on the back for your wisdom, and assure you that you are right and they are all wrong.

The Voice of Spirit, which is always "on," quietly reminds you that we are all the same, we come from the same Source, and we want the same things. Spirit will show you that *all* behavior is rooted in love; the "good" behavior is clearly demonstrating love, but that which we judge as "bad" behavior is nothing other than a *call for love*. The bad behavior is just the best way a person knows how to demonstrate that they are not experiencing love in that moment. If they did not know of love on some level, they would not know what they are missing, and so would not act out. A child only acts out if it is tired or missing comfort, food, or recognition. Essentially no difference.

Once I resolve to see the world and others as extensions of myself, each relationship in any circumstance becomes a portal to deeper Self-understanding, acceptance, and love. The end game here is that once we all "get it" on the level of Unity Consciousness, the next phase of planetary evolution will begin in earnest. Maybe only a small percentage of us have to consciously "get it" before a spontaneous wave of awakening overtakes the world. We have yet to fully come together and snap out of the spell of separation, but this is inevitable and is already happening. Our only real choice in the meantime is "How much longer do I want to suffer?" If I am truly done with suffering, then I am ready to embrace the Path of Forgiveness. On this path, giving becomes receiving. On this path, only love is real. All the rest is simply the illusion of love's absence. Because of my Divine inheritance, I have the power to bring love into any situation, past, present, or future.

There is great power to be released and realized in these understandings. At first, there can also be great confusion, as we realize the terrible cost of conditioned illusory thinking upon our own life's story and the collective human saga. We realize how needless the historical litany of human suffering has been, how pointless the centuries of war, struggle, and conflict have been, and all for naught . . . if we don't learn by them! We are so deeply entrenched in our judgments, many of which are upheld by institutions, "-isms," and generational beliefs weighed down by piles of moldy cultural baggage that we call "history."

The period of "reality adjustment" as we recognize our blindness and awaken to Universal Truth is called in some traditions the "dark night of the Soul." As the Soul is Divine and knows not of the dualistic concept of darkness, this period of adjustment is more accurately described as the "dark night of the ego." I would guess that a large number of folks who believe they are depressed are rather experiencing the early signs of Spiritual Awakening. You have to see the illusion for what it is and become "disillusioned"—this is a necessary step before you can embrace the reality hidden behind the veil. The "Spiritual emergence" movement in psychology is devoted to helping people through these early birth pains of the sudden onset of awareness. Researchers have discovered that many of our "diagnosed" conditions are natural reactions to sudden leaps of consciousness that simply need to be supported and assimilated into the former worldview and self-concept of the awakener.

Fear not, and try to remember to meditate before you medicate! Unlike chemical intervention, a crude and potentially harmful form of intervention based on a backward perception of causality, the choice to go into silence has no dangerous side effects and is freely available to all.

Please be encouraged that once the awakening has begun, like a pregnancy, it must come to fruition. There's no going back, and that's a good thing! We are not called to create a perfect future, as this is likely impossible here on Earth School. The future, as an aspect of the illusion of time, is being charted with each and every decision we make in this very moment. We are only called to respond to what is before us now. Trust: Spirit has your back, and will only lead to new "nows" that will build on and reinforce the peace you are accepting for yourself now.

It is most important to recognize that all Spirit is asking from you is your willingness to change. This will, which we have discussed as being One with Divine Will, is all that is required for the Divine Messenger to support you in every way you can perceive toward the goal that is given each of us. Spirit will accomplish this mission, even with as little as 1 percent willingness on your part; that's how willing and determined Spirit is to lead you home.

SEVENTEEN

True and False Forgiveness

As mentioned earlier, the mirror world has its own form of forgiveness which cannot work, as the dream world is a false image and literal reversal of everything true or real. In order to forgive according to the world's standards, forgiveness must have a reason or subject. This is true for most dualistic religions as well, particularly in their attachment to the concept of 'sin.' Dualistic religions are distracted by the false belief in "good *and* evil" as equally true and real. Many sincere believers become lopsided in their fanaticism to conquer evil and fail to address the illusion of separation and duality that gave birth to the concept of evil in the first place. Notice how "evil" is "live" spelled backward? See how the mirror world distorts life by convincing us we are inherently evil? No wonder dualistic religions have stood behind every "righteous war" and have been the keepers of "righteous indignation" against God's "enemies" over eons.

In its need for a subject and separate object, false for-giveness always operates on the premise that "I forgive you for _____." The world, and particularly the legal and religious systems, even entertains the ridiculous notion of the "unforgivable" sin used in order to justify murder, punishment, and war. Anyone smell ego?

The problem with applying forgiveness to a specific action or behavior is twofold. First, and most impor-tantly, it makes the bad behavior real and then, out of a sense of moral superiority, deigns to forgive it. We some-times off-handedly and superficially forgive in an attempt to relieve our own discomfort about a situation and get back to our unsure comfort zone of complacency. By first making the bad behavior real, do you think the ego's for-giveness also forgets? Not very likely. Rather, the ego's for-giveness is really saying, "I will forgive you because I am more pure and righteous than you, but I will never forget what you've done. I will constantly be on guard in case you try to pull that one again. I will always see you in light of what I forgave."

Which brings us to the second problem with false for-giveness: It maintains the separation between the forgiver and the forgiven. Do you see the ego's design in all of this? The ego is all for "righteous" action as long as someone is kept on the outside. Our entire justice system supports the permanent separation of "criminals" from the "law-abiding" population. It is a system based on the self-righteous desire to punish the evildoer seen as a symbolic projection of our own collective unconscious guilt. By separating out and punishing the offender, we stand in the false security of our own righteous image while soothing the unconscious suspicion that "There, but by the grace of God, go I."

We know false forgiveness does not work because it does not bear the fruit of peace or healed relationships. Any belief or behavioral pattern that keeps separation in place engenders fear. All our experiences around separation, from the most upsetting losses to the smallest slights, resonate with the only memory of separation that matters—the loss of knowledge of our Divinity at the point of the Big Bang. Every small separation experience recalls the ghost of the big separation. This is the only thing that truly needs forgiving, and here's the "cosmic joke" again: Because the separation did not really happen (only in a dream), *there is nothing in truth to forgive!* That's right. Forgiveness is in fact a temporary correction for something that didn't happen! True forgiveness is the final illusion that erases all the others that came before. By choosing to join in equality with another rather than maintain the false separation, we are facilitating the healing of ourselves, others, and the entire collective. Our reward is peace—something nothing in the world has the power to give us.

Forgiveness plus "something to forgive" is a dualistic concept. Realizing there is nothing real to forgive is a non-dual realization; the truth that sets everyone free. Truth is One, Illusions are legion. Truth is all-inclusive; illusions are specific. Only Truth is real.

Fortunately, the world has been offered a clear and practical historical example of non-dual forgiveness with the recent popularization of the traditional Hawaiian practice of Ho'oponopono (Ho-O-pono-pono).

HO'OPONOPONO: AN ANCIENT GIFT FOR MODERN TIMES

A fundamental principle in Spiritual healing is that there is nothing we necessarily need do to facilitate a Spiritual healing experience. It is not about "us" or our efforts in the usual sense of the word. More than an additive energy (yang), forgiveness is a release (yin). You are strongly encouraged to literally turn over each and every relationship to the Divine. Simply telling the Divine in your own heart, "This one's for you!" will do it. Then your ego has been put on notice and knows it is not welcome to jump in. You have hung up the internal sign that says "nobody home" to announce to the ego that you are not interested in its lame interpretation of reality, which is always wrong.

The simple forgiveness technique described here fits into any lifestyle or situation. Silently offer this as a prayer for the persons you will be relating to this day. Have it "running" in the background of your awareness as you give the other person your gentle and undivided attention, like offering a soft symphonic soundtrack in each moment. This gives the mind something to do while you cultivate inner silence, which is the one and only abode of Spirit.

Ho'oponopono is an ancient practice rooted in the traditional culture of Hawaii. In olden times, when a tribe or family member was in any kind of serious difficulty—illness, victim or perpetrator of crime, victim of a natural disaster, and so on, the whole family or tribe would gather around that person and silently search their own hearts for whatever role they may have played in this person's suffering. When each one came to an understanding, they would silently ask for forgiveness and then leave the circle. Eventually all that was left was one healed individual in the middle. Worked every time!

This ancient and venerable practice was an elegant example of quantum healing on the level of the One Mind, acting on the recognition that we are not separated, and that if you suffer within my perception, I share that suffering too. My perception of you as suffering is a projection of the suffering I still hold in my mind in the form of guilt. Otherwise I would only see you as you really are: Divine, innocent, and invulnerable. The results from this technique seem to confirm the theory that as we heal within ourselves, a spontaneous quantum wave of healing is created, which ripples outward and affects all.

Recently, a Hawaiian social worker, Dr. Hew Len, discovered that this technique worked equally well in modern institutional settings. Dr. Len found himself working the night shift in a hospital ward for the criminally insane. These were serious offenders, many of whom were shackled for their own and others' protection. Because Dr. Len did not have much else to do, he spent his nights alone, eventually recalling the ancient practice of his ancestors. He decided to adapt this ancient technique, which was passed on through his Mother's lineage, to his current situation. One by one, he would pull down each inmate's file, look at the picture, and simply repeat, "I love you, I am sorry, please forgive me, thank you" until he felt a lightness coming in when he regarded each picture. Without any other direct contact and by simply repeating this exercise night after night for a few months, Dr. Len saw *all the inmates get well* except a couple who were transferred to minimum security facilities. The hospital eventually shut down the ward, and Dr. Len was out of a job. Is this not the mark of a true healer?

Eventually, author Joe Vitale of *What the Bleep?* fame got wind of Dr. Len's work and wrote *Zero Limits*, an easy, inspiring read on this technique.[18] The form of forgiveness this practice offers is deceptively simple, yet profoundly powerful and transformative. As relationships are the key to our liberation, anything we can do to clear the unconscious guilt in the mind (which we project onto our relationships and experience as judgment) is the fastest way to heal the split in our own minds. Any time we feel a loss of peace and joy (our natural state) when we think of a person or situation, there is an opportunity to "clean" our own minds, as Dr. Len puts it. We can also apply the practice to objects, traffic jams, the evening news, or anything that comes into view that disturbs our peace, even in the slightest. Again, any disturbance we perceive is not in truth "out there" at all. When we react, we experience a

....

18. Joe Vitale, *Zero Limits* (Hoboken, NJ: John Wiley and Sons, 2007).

part of ourselves that still clings to our belief in separation, and thus fear, guilt, and pain.

Eventually, you can internalize the intent and shorten the words to "I love you, thank you." You can be "running" the words even while you are engaged in conversation, or any time at all! With past relationships, all we need to do to connect is hold a picture of the person in our minds as we direct the intentions. We are connecting via the "psychic internet" that connects us all on the level of One Mind.

Note: You do not have to "feel" true forgiveness. Just be willing to give it a try. The good feeling comes later as a reward for the willingness to forgive. We are sometimes reluctant to give up the ego payoff our resentment offers. Even if you are just willing to be willing, that is enough. That is all the opening Spirit needs to go to work!

It is still possible to practice Ho'oponopono without the deeper insight of a non-dual perspective. I sense that if you hold a non-dual understanding as you say the words, the power of the technique is vastly increased. Here is the deeper non-dual meaning behind what you are saying when you practice Ho'oponopono:

"*I love you.* I include you as part of my Self. I respect you and give you total freedom to be who you are and to make your own decisions about what lessons you need to learn. I rejoice in our Oneness, as I know your healing is my healing. To not love you is to not love myself."

"*I am sorry* . . . for the role I have played in your suffering in choosing, along with you and everyone, the experience of separation. I know there is really only one problem: the belief in separation. Therefore, I bear the burden and share the responsibility for your suffering, which is my suffering too."

"*Please forgive me*. To forgive means literally to "overlook." I ask you to join me and overlook the impossible. I accept that the belief in separation at the root of all suffering is nothing other than an illusion. I ask you to see me in my innocence, which is who I truly am, as I see you in yours. Please overlook our belief in illusions, and release us both from the prison of judgment. There is only One of us here. I trust you to love me, for I know who you really are."

"*Thank you* for the opportunity to heal the unconscious guilt in my mind, your mind, and in the One Mind we share. For it is only because I carry this guilt that I can perceive any fault in you. You have acted as my mirror, and in receiving your forgiveness, I extend it in love back to you."

Ho'oponopono is a precious gift, "held in waiting," as it were, by the Hawaiian culture for this time of transformation. Many students of prehistory believe that Hawaii is a remnant of an ancient society that predates Atlantis. It was a very spiritually evolved society. If so, it makes sense that the Hawaiians would have a practice involving the greatest spiritual gift we can offer anyone.

It is only through True Forgiveness, which ultimately leads to the knowing "there is nothing real to forgive," that we can heal the schisms on this planet between people, races, nations, and with Earth herself. Choosing the path of forgiveness in this life is the greatest gift you give to yourself and everyone here. It is also the best guarantee of your own happiness—fulfilling this purpose, the healing of all, is the greatest source of deep, enduring joy. It is a time for total amnesty . . . the past is over, and the future unburdened of the past beckons. Forgiveness is our fastest ticket and "golden doorway" out of the dream of duality and back to the real world awaiting us all beyond the veil of separation.

FORGIVING YOURSELF

This can be the hardest form of forgiveness, as the ego is so invested in keeping you down! It literally is battling for its own (pseudo) life, and will destroy you in body rather than see you released to your true freedom. Of course, as we have seen, forgiveness of others is self-forgiveness at the core, so if you have accepted the Path of Forgiveness you have also started the process of self-forgiveness. What if there is one burning issue or memory that the ego loves to bring up out of the blue to ensure that you stay unawakened to your Divine Self? That "terrible" thing you did in the eyes of others, society, or religion is nothing other than a false mental image of yourself as less than perfect, as you were created. Nevertheless, you can adapt the practice of Ho'oponopono to address yourself. Simply hold a mental image of yourself at the time of the "unforgivable" event, or find a picture of yourself from around that time, and simply do as Dr. Len did. Any past relationship can be healed in the same manner; the past is not "fixed" by any means. The past is only ever a present-time memory made up of images and judgments we formed in the moment from our level of awareness at the time. By going back and making a decision to forgive rather than condemn, we literally rewrite the experience and change all outcomes to match a higher level of awareness. You become a "time master"! Time no longer imprisons you. Rather, by using it for the new purpose of forgiveness, time serves your return to the knowledge of your Divine and Innocent Self, which is far beyond the limits of all time, space, or bodies.

You might want to start a "forgiveness list" of all those who spring to mind. Any relationship that causes your energy level to drop when you think of it is a candidate for this work. You may find that some relationships require frequent "cleaning" until no trace of guilt remains. This will depend on the depth of the original guilt this person represents; the deeper the injury, the deeper the healing opportunity. And, because we are all truly One, any completely healed relationship resonates in the quantum field and clears the way for the eventual healing of all relationships. This was the gift of Christ in the form of the historical figure Jeshua Ben Joseph (Jesus), who opened the door to the complete healing of the One Mind by his unwavering and uncompromising will to forgive, even toward those who were destroying his body.

Physical death is the ace up the ego's sleeve. Those who are only body-identified must fear the oblivion physical death symbolizes for them. As the game progresses, however, we find there is no death and the ace was only a bluff. Thousands of documented near-death experiences by credible sources now attest to the unreality of death as the end of anything but the body. Oh yes, it is the end of taxes too, at least until the next incarnation! Physical death is a transition of energy from one state to another. There is nothing real to fear.

You are now in planetary service as you embark on this highest Path of Healing. The Course promises that "all relationships are eventually healed." It's really just a matter of time—time being part of the illusion. By starting today, you have already begun to save time and reduce suffering which is all we truly accomplish here. True Forgiveness is the supreme lesson that Earth School has to offer. Two thousand years ago, the world at large was not ready for this message. Are we ready now? Do we really have a choice?

Starting Over

We have come a long way together in our attempt to set straight some ideas about life, happiness, reality, and all those big-picture themes. When it comes down to it, though, life is only ever lived in this moment. So the experience of this moment is where any journey begins and ends. I hope this moment is an accurate reflection of who you truly are—a moment of love and acceptance, of comfort and peace. If it isn't, put this book down right now, and go within. What you want is already yours, waiting for you to discover where you misplaced it. After that, if you so choose, you may read this book again. After all, words, like relationships, are only mirrors of yourself. Having come this far, I think you will see this book through fresh eyes and at deeper levels upon a second read, for in truth the beauty and wonder that is you is beyond any limit we have imagined.

Like all of us, you will occasionally stumble. You may fall back into old patterns and repeat the same mistakes again and again. But there will be one big difference when you do—you will know you were not acting from your Self, only from ego. You were simply out of your right mind. And because now the ego is exposed and disappearing, you will no longer condemn yourself when you stumble. You simply pick yourself up, dust off, and begin again with a light heart and joyful anticipation of all that is yours forever. I am so pleased to be on this journey with you. Thank you for joining me, and helping me become complete.

I love you. I am sorry for forgetting that sometimes. Please forgive me for falling asleep. Thank you for being part of my dream. Shall we wake up now?

About the Author

David Ian Cowan is a biofeedback trainer and teacher in spiritual communication and the art of dowsing. He is a counselor, alternative health practitioner and trainer living in Boulder, Colorado. He is also the author of *Navigating the Collapse of Time* (Weiser Books, 2011) and co-author with Erina Cowan of *Dowsing Beyond Duality* (Weiser Books, 2013).

Visit him at *www.bluesunenergetics.net*.

To Our Readers

Weiser Books, an imprint of Red Wheel/Weiser, publishes books across the entire spectrum of occult, esoteric, speculative, and New Age subjects. Our mission is to publish quality books that will make a difference in people's lives without advocating any one particular path or field of study. We value the integrity, originality, and depth of knowledge of our authors.

Our readers are our most important resource, and we appreciate your input, suggestions, and ideas about what you would like to see published.

Visit our website at *www.redwheelweiser.com* to learn about our upcoming books and free downloads, and be sure to go to *www.redwheelweiser.com/newsletter* to sign up for newsletters and exclusive offers.

You can also contact us at *info@rwwbooks.com* or at

Red Wheel/Weiser, LLC
665 Third Street, Suite 400
San Francisco, CA 94107